Never eat Stink Bait

Lessons Learned from the Creek Bank

Never eat Stink Bait

Lessons Learned from the Creek Bank

BRYAN MELLAGE

FLAT FISH
PUBLISHING, LLC

Auburn, Nebraska

Never eat Stink Bait

Inquiries: www.FlatFishPublishing.com

FLAT FISH
PUBLISHING, LLC

Paperback: 978-1-7332306-1-2

Mobi: 978-1-7332306-2-9

EPUB: 978-1-7332306-3-6

Library of Congress Cataloging Number: 2019908375

Cataloging in Publication Data on file with Publisher

Publishing and production by Concierge Marketing Inc.

Illustrations by Kirsten Meier

Printed in the United States of America

10 9 8 7 6 5 4 3 2 1

To Carrie:

There are not enough
Thank You's in "Thanks" to
say how much I appreciate all
your help and encouragement.

Thank you!

Contents

Introduction

A long time ago in a land far, far away—shall we say Nebraska—there lived a mild-mannered man. Let's call him Bryan.

The dirt floor log cabin that was situated high up in the bluffs overlooking the Missouri River, where the metamorphosis from youthful pup to old dog took place, made him into the man that he is today. He is a chiseled man, rock hard, with a mind like a steel trap. His hunting and fishing lore is known throughout the area. He is said to be able to smell when a fish is about to bite, hear a mushroom poking up through the forest floor, and outwit even the wiliest of whitetails. He can remember the secret locations of every fishing hole, game trail and hidden mushroom field. People worshipfully just call him "Sage."

We have all heard that perception is reality. Well, there is a lot of "perceptioning" going on in that paragraph.

The reality is: I find myself in front of the clothes drawer, standing in my underwear, trying to remember what I forgot.

The reality is: going hunting and forgetting my gun.

The reality is: when I look into the mirror—I see this old wrinkled man, whom I cannot recognize, looking back at me. I feel good on days when I can remember two out of four of my children's names.

The truth of my story, which is sometimes hard to come by, is that I had a childhood that Mark Twain could have written about. I was blessed with the guiding force of a mother and father who did not see a problem using the back of the hand to help me stay straight on my journey. Having loving parents who helped instill the life skills of being honest, working hard and being thankful for each day you get to walk this land was the best gift I have been given and one that I have worked to give to my children.

The reality is I grew up in a small Norman Rockwellian abode on the edge of a small rural town. There was no dirt floor. Not to say that the floor of our house did not have dirt on it. No matter how many times my mother told me to wipe my feet as I ran into the house through the back door, I never remembered to do it. Mud or not. Sometimes it was not the back of the hand either, but the full force of motherly education with a fly swatter on my forgetful rear end that helped to jog my memory.

It was not a big house, but it was a home. A home that was full of love and affection. Dad's job keeping farm equipment and trucks running did not provide a lavish lifestyle, but we always had everything we needed. But there is not undue perception of the fact that growing up in Southeast Nebraska was a great place to be a kid. Every day that I was not forced to sit behind a desk in school, whether it was in the classroom or in the principal's office, I would be outside. On Saturdays and every day of the summer, I would jump out of bed, launch myself out the back door, and be gone for the rest of the day, except maybe for a moment for a quick bite to eat for more fuel to continue the journey of exploring the world around me.

The outdoors was a big place, and it took all day to see it. It was an easy process of scheduling. Whenever I got hungry or got hurt, when I got tired or it got dark, I went home.

The advantage of living in the small town was not evident to me as a small lad, but it was there. Everyone knew everyone, and everyone was watching. It did not matter that your mom could not see you; every mother in town could see you and report back to the main office on what you had done. I now know it was part of the gift I was given as a person growing up in a small town and was also the same gift my children had in their childhood. They did not understand until later how I knew what they had done before they even got home.

Small rural-town living meant you waved at everyone. You knew most of the people you saw, and even if you didn't know them, they were waving hello to you anyway.

Growing up, hunting and fishing were as much of a part of the routine as summer Vacation Bible School and back-yard-in-the-tent sleepovers were.

As the years went by, the fake cowboy cap pistols and games of Cowboys and Indians were replaced by a .22 rifle and rabbit hunting. A quick walk out our back door, and I would be walking a tree line, with my single-shot small bore rifle, hunting imaginary big game.

My friends and I spent endless days and nights camping along creek banks and little ponds or mosquito-infested timbers, believing we were lost in time and space. We were having the time of our lives, living the dream the people in the big cities could only fantasize about.

Every area of the world experiences weather swings and has stories to describe them. But in Nebraska, our weather fluctuations are monumental—almost Biblical. Ice fishing in the morning, then wearing short sleeves and mowing the lawn in the afternoon are considered normal.

Another part of living in Nebraska involves football. Everyone drives a vehicle that has a big red N on it. On home game days, Memorial Stadium in Lincoln is the third largest city in the state. Growing up, on Saturday game day for Nebraska football meant you were sitting in front of the three station, black and white TV, and if the game was not televised, you were listening to the fading in and out static-filled sound of Lyell Bremser's voice calling the game on the AM radio.

All in all, growing up in the wilderness of Southeast Nebraska was about the best thing that has ever happened to me. The memories of my childhood are some of my most cherished treasures.

To fish or not to fish

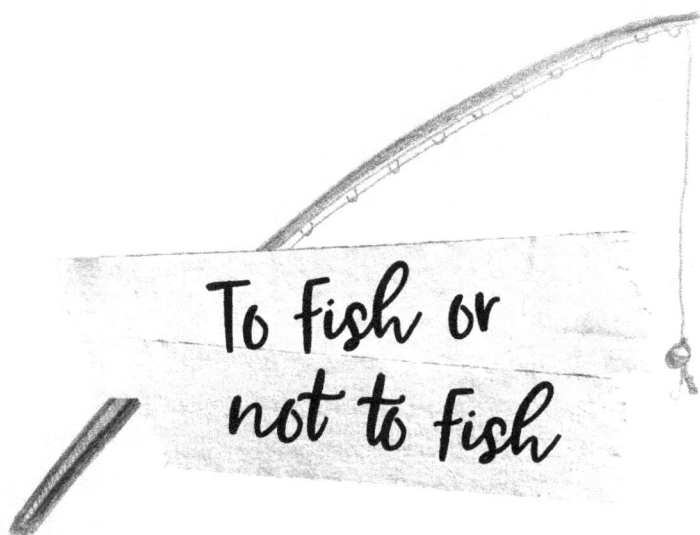

There are many great dilemmas in life. Obstacles to overcome; decisions to make. Any well-educated person can debate quantum physics, the theory of relativity, or cold fusion. But for the working man—the horde of us who have to shoulder the task of supporting the rest of the world—we cannot waste our time on such frivolous notions; we have bigger fish to fry. We must contemplate the most complex of man's problems. Should I get married, should I have another beer—should I fish?

Ever since man put the welcome mat in front of the cave, it has been our duty to feed the family. From the time we first dangled a willow branch over a quiet pool to present an offering to the finned ones in the water, it has been the man's job to go to the creek and bring home dinner. Those were the good ole days.

We had not yet been told that we had to be sensitive, and try to understand our female companions. The meaning of

"Keeping up with the neighbors" was translated into running faster than them to keep from becoming the saber-toothed tiger's next meal. A good loin cloth and a sharp spear were all that was needed to face the day. But, of course, those were easier times.

In today's world on a daily basis, we must march off to the factory. For without us, who would tighten the bolt, sweep the floor and make the next widget? If we were not there to flip the switch, to man the station, the whole fabric of our world might collapse. This is a big responsibility to bear.

Yet, if left to our own, we would go fishing. But who would cut the lawn, trim the bushes and keep up with the Joneses?

The calluses on the hands and soreness in the muscles mean that we are the backbone, the heart and soul of the engine we call economics. We cannot take a day off; the nation is depending on us to stand our post.

Civilization has tried to take away our fishing mentality. It is still there, but we must keep it in the back corner of the garage.

Maybe it is time to rethink our position in this grand picture. So let's ponder the act of fishing and how it interacts with the rest of the world.

What is fishing? Fishing is the act of obtaining the gear needed in pursuit of a quarry—the ever wary, highly elusive, and mythical fish. First, we need a glittering' speckled, bigger than you will ever need, high horsepower fishing boat. This floating fish-catching machine will have to be equipped with the latest and best offerings in fish finders, depth finder and GPS. Of course, we will need hooks, line, bobbers, reels, tackle boxes, sinkers, pliers, net, and let's not forget the beer cooler. Rods, oh yes, rods. Depending on spring or fall, bluegill or mighty catfish, walleye or bass, if it has gills and swims; it is our station in life to pursue it. We are obligated to have in our mandatory list of equipment rod and reel combinations for crappie, a tackle box for lake fishing, big river tackle, and all the best Bass Pro and Cabelas can offer to bring Mr. Bass to the boat.

I have not even mentioned lures. A person could spend four years in higher education to completely understand the full complexity of what it takes to entice a cold-blooded, finned, simple-brained animal to try and swallow your lure. Not just any lure, but a brightly colored, striped, spotted, bait-resembling, noise-making lure. We will be obliged to drag along several tackle boxes to carry the full assortment of specific fish-enticing lures, requiring several trips to the boat just for your lures.

The colors and designs of these lures have been thoroughly investigated and scientifically tested to catch the interest of even the most wary quarry, and they have demonstrated their ability to do the job—they caught us, didn't they?

Not that we would ever admit to our wives how much we have spent for all this equipment; it all has attached value—a sticker price. I had a friend tell me that his biggest fear was that his wife would sell all his fishing equipment after he died for what he told her he bought it for.

The almighty dollar is at the center of the capitalist system. Money is the fuel that drives the U.S. economy, and the money spent on fishing equipment is essential to the wellbeing of the whole system. It could be conjured that without our purchases of indispensable fishing equipment, the whole house of cards might collapse.

It is our duty. Our country needs us.

So, break the cookie jar and head to the local sports shop and lay down that greenback—who needs a new washing machine? Buy all that is needed to bring that fish to the net.

As for myself, for the common good, as an American, and patriot—I will fish.

Fishing Partner

The world has seen some great duos throughout the generations. Unions like Batman and Robin, Bert and Ernie, Fred and Barney, Yogi and Boo-Boo Bear are synonymous with cohesive companionship cooperation. Similar is the union of me and the Redhead. We have been married now since the last ice age. Although there have been volumes of words used, I honestly do not remember anyone using the particular word "cohesive" to describe our relationship.

But a fishing partner is another whole higher level of companionship. This goes beyond working together or just spending time with another person. Fishing partners deal on an ESP-intellectual level. We know what the other is thinking and what he is going to do next without being told. The thoughts from your fishing partner enter your body through osmosis. There is no longer the need for spoken words between fishing partners—just brain waves connecting two in-sync individuals.

Let me explain.

My brother-in-law, Gar-Bob, and I have been fishing together since we were kids. Long before I noticed Gar-Bob's redheaded little sister.

For example, Gar-Bob and I are meandering along the riverbank looking for a likely place to sit and throw a line. It is hot out—stifling hot—the kind of heat that keeps most sane people inside. There is no wind, nothing to remove the intense heat from your body. The sun's rays are leaving burn marks on my fragile skin. My eyes are stinging from the sweat running into them. I am thinking to myself, what is wrong with Gar-Bob today? Why did he want to go fishing today anyway, especially now, in the middle of the day in this broiler oven heat?

This is stupid, I grumble to myself. We should be back at Gar-Bob's fish shack, sitting in front of the window-mounted little noisemaker he calls an AC unit, sucking up the semi-cool air it generates, waiting for the cool of the night to come out here, with my hand tightly holding a cold beverage.

Continuing on, we round a bend in the river and are confronted with a long, lazy sand bar. We trek across this little stretch of Sahara. We have the demon sun sending out asphalt-deforming heat from above, and now we have the added pleasure of the reflective warmth from beneath us. I can feel the soles on my shoes and my toenails melting in unison.

But as the river bends here, it has formed an eddy along the far bank. I stop, looking out to that spot, thinking that if I were a fish, that is where I would be. I glance back at Gar-Bob, who is staring at the same spot I am. He turns back to me and tilts his head in the direction of the small whirlpool that is riding on top of the spot in the river that we should throw our lines to.

Without a word spoken, we had chosen the same spot, at the same time. We are truly partners on a playing field most only hope to get to.

I kick my shoes off and step out into the water a wee bit, trying to combat the skin-deforming heat. I throw my line in and begin what I am sure will be a short wait until I get a bite and catch the first fish.

The first few minutes drag into the first half hour. I sneak a peek at Gar-Bob from the corner of my eye. He is standing stoically there, holding his fishing pole—not moving, intent on his task, a coiled spring waiting for a fish to bite.

The next half hour becomes an hour and still not a single nibble.

Gar-Bob is still at attention. He has not moved. I am not sure, but I think he is standing up asleep. Not a murmur coming from him. The heat has turned him into a kiln-fired statue.

I reel in my line several times, check my bait, and throw my line back out, moving it a few feet either way, thinking I might not have placed my offering in the exact spot needed to have Mr. Fish find it. But nothing. It is just too darned hot.

It's about two hours before I reach my heat-exhaustion limit.

I make a loud noise that echoes off everything surrounding us. I clear my throat several times before Gar-Bob wakes from his fishing trance and looks back at me.

"Time da leave?" Gar-Bob booms.

I nod in affirmation.

Without any words to clutter the moment, Gar-Bob and I silently head back to the road and our pickup.

After we safely stowed (chucked) our fishing gear into the back of the pickup, we climb into the front seat. My shirt is wringing from the sweat my body has poured out during our excursion. Getting into the pickup was much easier than I remember it being the last time. Then it hits me: I am now many pounds lighter. It is going to take gallons of water to replace what I lost today.

It takes a few moments to recoup the energy lost over the last couple of hours. I sit panting. I feel flushed. I look into the rearview mirror and see my face has changed to a few shades of roasted lobster. The tops of my ears are bright red.

I look toward Gar-Bob, whose intent look is an unnerving glare right back at me. I feel like the last piece of pizza after the Weight Watchers meeting.

"What the blue blazes was that all about?" Gar-Bob growls. "Fishing out there on that sandbar, with no shade. You couldn't find a better place—someplace with a tree to sit under?" He continued with a fury borne of the radiant heat we had been standing in for the last two hours.

"We fished there because you nodded your head toward that piece of river," I replied in a low, scratchy voice, my vocal cords feeling like pieces of string that had been barbecued.

"There is no way I would have stopped to fish there. If you hadn't stopped there, I would have kept walking, and besides that, why were we out there in the first place? It was like an oven out there. I felt like a piece of cut fish being cooked in bubbling oil."

"What…What are you talking about?" I stammered, "We were out there because you…YOU wanted to go fishing," pointing my sun-burned hand at him.

"Me? Did a rabid dog bite you? I wanted to just stay at the f'shin' shack, sit in front of the AC, drinkin' a cold one." Gar-Bob roared.

See, that is what I am talking about!

Fishing partners, completely in tune with one another. We both wanted to do the exact same thing.

Fishing partners spend a lot of time together. Sure, the Redhead and I are married, but between working for the man, fishing, hunting, cleaning game and getting ready to go fishing and hunting, about the only real time I am able to spend with, and talk to the little woman is at night when I ask her what vittles she is cooking for dinner.

Unlike the Redhead, who never says derogatory things to me (I hope that she does not read this), fishing partners can be cruel and say things that can be hurtful because they do not feel the need to worry about your feelings. They speak from the gut—honest and holding nothing back.

Gar-Bob and I were out on my boat fishing on the river recently. Gar-Bob sticks his fingers into a jar of rotting shad pieces, pulling out a slimy, stinking slab of fish cut bait, leaving a stench about the area that is attracting varmints from miles away. The aroma lingers like a toxic cloud, until it floats over to my side of the boat where I am sitting, and it violently scalds my nose hairs all the way to the back in my sinuses. By violently, I mean it feels like someone clamped little vise grips on the hairs and viciously yanked them out, one by one.

These nose hairs must be connected to the back side of my eyeballs, because now my pupils are smashed into the back of my eye sockets, stuck there. My eyelids are permanently jammed into the open position. My back is straight, the brim on my hat has gone limp, and I am no longer breathing. My survival instincts are keeping me from inhaling a new barrage of stench.

Let me explain—this is no ordinary jar of shad. This is Gar-Bob's secret catfish bait made from ingredients that read like a witch's brew. Lizard tongue, bat's ear, hair of troll and other forbidding elements I do not want to think about.

He lets this all sit in a Mason jar in direct sun light until the jar lid swells up and looks to be about ready to pop off. Gar-Bob says you can tell if the stink bait is done. "It'll cr'wl out of the jar and impale itself onto your hook on its own."

The added benefit of Gar-Bob's cut bait is that not only is it ranked as one of the top ten of the most disgusting smells on Earth, it is also caustic.

Gar-Bob has whispered the rumor that he has sold his cut bait recipe to the Government. Gar-Bob says the CIA uses it

NEVER EAT STINK BAIT

to dissolve the fingerprints off of their secret agents. When I am using Gar-Bob's bait, I have to be careful not to drip any of it onto the bottom of the boat, for it would burn a hole right through it.

After Gar-Bob has put some of this catfish fare on his hook and thrown it into the water, he does what every man does—wipes his fingers on his pants. That way that stinging smell stays with us in the boat for the rest of the afternoon.

I have heard Gar-Bob's wife ask him, "How do you get all these holes in your jeans?"

Gar-Bob's next task is to rig another pole; it needs a new hook tied onto the end of the line. He holds the line, it is frayed, so he licks his fingers—let me repeat that, he licks his fingers, so he can wet the fishing line so it will go through the eye of the hook better. After that, the show started.

Gar-Bob's tongue begins to aggressively move in and out of his mouth, obviously trying to use his lips and teeth to scrape something off his tongue.

He coughs a few times, and then gags, his eyes blink like taillights with a weak flasher, and then he goes into an epileptic episode, shaking his head back and forth, attempting to regain a normal reality. I think his head might start spinning like a top.

After a few moments of trying to get the taste out of his mouth, the second sales feature of Gar-Bob's cut bait kicks in, as it begins to scorch his taste buds.

He spends several seconds savagely licking his shirt sleeve. He is past trying to get the substance off his tongue; he has been reduced to trying to just remove the top layer of his tongue.

BRYAN MELLAGE

He drinks all the water we have brought along with us and looks for anything else to pour into his mouth.

(It is truly an enjoyable scene to watch. Fishing partners enjoy the macabre.)

Now, all the giggling and jocularity I have been doing has awakened a sleeping dragon in my gut. I can feel a rustling deep down in my stomach. Last night's meal does not seem to like the hardy belly laughing that I have been doing as I watch Gar-Bob writhe in agony. The turmoil going on deep down within the core of my body foretells an epic struggle about to begin.

When a volcano builds up pressure, it will blow its top and send the pressure, smoke and smells up in a deadly plume.

Humans vent from the other end. I wait until the pressure gets to the breaking point, lean to the side a little to give the forces within me an escape route, and let the noxious plume go. There is a lot more built-up pressure than I had anticipated, and the fact that I was already leaning to one side was nearly my downfall. I was almost flung over the side of the boat.

My plume did not have a smell rivaling Gar-Bob's cut bait, but there was a new aroma in the boat with us.

Gar-Bob's face became all wrenched and twisted up; he gave me a look of disbelief and sarcastically said, "That is just plain disgusting."

"Really, that is what you think is disgusting?"

The façade I tried to portray of being hurt by his remarks was cancelled out by the cynical smile on my face.

One night Gar-Bob and I were sitting out in front of his fish shack. We were lounging in the 1970's vintage nylon—

wrapped aluminum frame lawn chairs that he had dug out of someone's trash. You cannot buy that kind of ambiance from eBay. The AC unit was really vibrating that night, making more noise than usual, and the amount of barely-a-few-degrees-below-warm air emitting from it was not worth the abuse to our ears.

While we were sitting there, a younger woman came by with a graceful stride, being led by a scroungy brown mutt of a dog on a leash. Now, I am old enough that "younger" means anyone not carrying an AARP card, but this woman is decades from worrying about wrinkles and retirement. She had long, tanned legs topped off with brightly colored short shorts, a tank top that stopped at her mid-section showing off her shiny belly button ring. Her shoulder-length, dishwater blonde hair was flowing in the slight evening breeze.

As I let my eyes follow this sight traveling in front of us, I hear, "Pstssh" as Gar-Bob pops the tab on a cold beer. Without turning my head away from the spectacle, I reach out for the replacement brew Gar-Bob is handing me.

"Sure is a nice dog," Gar-Bob states matter-of-factly.

Fishing partners to the end, on the same page, thinking the same thing.

Fishing the River

Nebraska is one of the true treasures that the United States has bestowed on its citizens. In all of Nebraska, the best place to be is here in the southeast corner of the state. Living down here where Nebraska bumps into Kansas, Missouri, and Iowa, we have the destinations, people and ambiance that make it the finest place to live, and one of the top reasons for a fisherman to dwell here is the Missouri River. My brother-in-law, Gar-Bob, and I can leave the fishing shack and the world of landlubbers and be floating in the Missouri River in ten minutes.

For instance, my wife says, "I want to see you out in the yard mowing grass by the top of the hour." I can be sitting, leaning back in the cushionless front seat of the boat, pole in hand, yelling at Gar-Bob for a cold one long before she has even gone out in the yard looking for me.

The exciting thing about the Missouri River is that not only can you catch monster catfish, but on any given day, you can also catch walleye, crappie, northern pike, sturgeon, and other assorted fish. If you want to drive around in circles, you can entice some Chinese silver carp to jump into your boat. However, usually they will hit you upside the head first, before falling and flopping to the bottom of the boat.

Everyone has visions of fish jumping into the boat and going home with a "boat load" without even wetting a line. But the invasion of the Chinese carp has not been a fishing dream come true. When Gar-Bob came back from fishing on the river with stories of fish literally jumping into his boat, I just put it in the category of "Gar-Bob Fish Stories."

The first time I was able to personally witness these flying fish, I was easing the family yacht (which looks a lot like a beat up ole flat bottom jon boat) up into the mouth of the Little Nemaha River, where it empties its load into

NEVER EAT STINK BAIT

the Missouri. My dad was out in the front of the boat, and another river rat friend of mine, Red, was in the middle. One of the Chinese silver carp launched itself out of the water, totally airborne, and went clear across the boat just missing the back of my dad's head and passing right in front of Red's crooked nose. They say the silver carp are scared by the noise made by the engine and prop, their natural evasion instincts kick in, and they jump out of the water to avoid whatever they think is chasing them. I hate to tell them, but my little 25-horsepower Merc is no threat to them; they could just slowly swim away.

Well, Red—who has been blindsided many times, and I can take credit for many of those—was obviously wound up about a 20 pound soaring fish trying to fly into his ear. Red said, "Did you see that?"

My dad turned around and said, "What?" Red told him that a fish had just jumped out of the water and flew from one side of the boat to the other and had just missed the back of his head. My dad's response, in a very disbelieving tone was, "Well, give me a drink!"

The result of that excursion was that I had to go back to Gar-Bob and admit that he was right. That left a bad taste in my mouth for nearly a month.

There is a misconceived belief in our local area that Gar-Bob and I, and the river rat gang I hang out with, have some all-knowing, mystical, spiritual oneness with the river. It is seemingly egged on by the fact that Gar-Bob tells everybody down at the local watering hole that.

But in all reality, the river is like a wife. I have been married for the time it has taken for all my hair to fall off my head and to reappear growing out of my ears, my eyesight to diminish and my hearing to fade away—which can be deceiving. I can hear a squirrel running across the forest floor and cannot hear my wife yelling at me from the other room, which is kind of strange. Even though the decades have passed since I uttered the phrase, "I do," or as I later learned, "Yes, Dear, I will do whatever you want." I am still learning about my wife and my place and duties in this organization.

The Missouri River has similar qualities. I learn something every time I go out on its flowing water. One always has to understand that the river is in charge and you are just being allowed to float on its surface. One of the problems of having people telling you that you have some sage-like river knowledge is that you can begin to believe it yourself.

Not only can the Missouri River be mysterious and cagey, it can also be like my redheaded wife and demoralize you with a deer-in-the-headlights look of "What just happened?" One minute calm and placid, and the next the river is a heavy-weight boxer looking to take your head off. Like I said—just like being married.

Nebraska is blessed with a lot of water moving across the state, and it all eventually goes by my back door, down the Missouri River on its way to the gulf. Western Nebraska had received record rainfall that was flowing or should I say, raging down the Platte River toward its inevitable meeting with the Missouri River, and my corner of the state. I get a

NEVER EAT STINK BAIT

call from Gar-Bob. He had been doing some mathematical calculations, and he was trying to explain them to me, which can be compared to to Elmer Fudd giving a lecture to Daffy Duck on Einstein's Theory of Relativity.

He said, "We all know that the fish bite better when the water is rising."

I had to agree with him on this tried-and-true fishing fact. His math went something like this: river current is about seven miles per hour, and the water from Western Nebraska has to travel x. We are the constant y, and we should be out on the river right now catching fish. With our precise calculations of when the river will come up, and when we should be back at the boat dock, all will be just dandy. Our keen Lewis & Clark-like understanding of the Missouri River meant our success was already written.

Now my first alarm should have gone off with "Y" are we going out on the river when a flood is coming?

So, within the hour we are tied up to a wing dike, poles hanging on the rod holders, line in the water waiting for Moby Dick to find us. As darkness began to cover us, I noticed what looked to be debris floating down the river. Now, as the first mate, it was my job to report this observation, which I did.

Gar-Bob, captain of the vessel and the brains of the operation, said, "Can't be, it's gunnabe a couple more hours before the flood will git here."

Even though we were confident of our math skills, we decided to head back to the boat dock. When we got out into the current, it became instantly obvious that we had messed up our x's and y's. The river was completely full of floating sticks, branches, limbs and assorted other timber.

BRYAN MELLAGE

I asked Gar-Bob for the spotlight and he said, "Spotlight? What light? I thought you brought the light?"

The quote from *Jaws*, "You're gonna need a bigger boat" rolled around in my head, I scurried around in the dark until I found a light under the steering wheel console. I turned on the spotlight, which Dollar General calls an "economy flashlight," and the area of the boat from in front of the steering wheel all the way to the first oar lock dimly lit up. I hoped that the search and rescue team had a better light.

As first mate, I had to get up in the front of the boat. I felt like one of the sculptured women on the front of an 18th century wooden sail boat, and we were going up an unexplored section of the Amazon. With the subpar rays of light probing the darkness, my job was to spot the potential prop-destroying objects and yell, "Go right" or "go left," back to the bridge. Even though Gar-Bob and I were only a few feet apart, at times, this only left just enough time between when I saw the log, screamed the instructions, and Gar-Bob yanked on the steering wheel to miss it.

We zig-zagged up the river like a destroyer trying to shake a U-boat. We were going upstream at the speed of hair growing, trying to get back to the boat dock, when even with my diminished light, I could tell there was something to the left of us, and to the right of us, and it was also above us. It was a tree, a floating lumber yard, a complete full-grown Herculean wooden battleship that was big enough to build the wife a new house, equipped with the four bathrooms she always wanted, and more than big enough to defeat us.

I turned around and with hurricane potency yelled at Gar-Bob, "BACK UP!" The force blew his hat off, only his fearful grip on the steering wheel keeping him in the boat.

The prop dug in and the branches of the tree began to engulf us. I said hello to a family of squirrels. I took the time to pick a few acorns, and finally the boat pulled away from the oaken tentacles.

Eventually we arrived safely back at the boat dock. We loaded up and headed home. Neither of us said much. Every once in a while, I would throw a glance at Gar-Bob. I made my best Superman face, squinted my eyes and tried to burn holes in his head with my laser beams, but it did not work.

I stumbled through the back door of the house. I felt like getting down on the ground and kissing the floor. One of my children ran up to me and said, "I am having trouble with my math homework. Can you help me?"

I kept on walking.

If you want to know about fishing on the Missouri River, my advice is to buy a book.

Floating down the river

My brother-in-law, Gar-Bob, and I have spent a great deal of time fishing out on the Missouri River together. Its meandering flow forms the eastern edge of my home state of Nebraska. Sitting in our boat, we can look out across the "Big Muddy" to the east, at the poor devils who are forced to reside in Iowa and Missouri. I guess their pioneer forefathers could not figure out how to get their wagons across the river.

Our forefathers, on the other hand, had the savvy and wherewithal to cross the wide expanse of the river, only then to have the wheel come off the wagon, and with that decided to plant their stakes here on the western side of the river and "Voila!" Nebraska was born.

Nebraska's first communities were river towns that sprang up along the Missouri River. Transportation was the key. The river was the interstate highway of the day.

When cruising up the river, one can still feel the presence of those who have come this way, with some minor differences.

What I remember from my history class—besides the sound of the ruler hitting my desk—was that Lewis & Clark had to persuade their boats up-river with oars, and even with ropes pulled from the bank. That reads a lot like work to me. I think I would have been one of those standing on the river bank, waving goodbye, and giggling to myself as they left St. Louis.

Gar-Bob and I have a distinct advantage over Lewis and Clark. We have a map of the river, and on most days no one shoots arrows at us from the bank. With our mighty outboard motor powerplant bolted to the transom of our beat-up, flat-bottom aluminum jon boat, Gar-Bob and I could have sprinted around the Discovery Team and left them in our massive wake.

I say sprint rather loosely. Our old boat engine was not built with any extra horsepower. There are just 35 of them, and some of the horses are not as high-spirited as they once were, and one has to remember all 35 of them are really old horses.

Our boat motor does not have all the fancy, frivolous options that the big boys have. Our old Evinrude is a tried and tested version. For those who have cashed in their winning lottery ticket and purchased a new expensive boat, let them beware. All those fru fru buttons to electronically start the engine, make the electric choke and electric tilt work, and the automatic oiler for the fuel injection motor will eventually go bad and fail, and then where will they be?

Gar-Bob and I do not have to worry about such problems. After a short half hour of prodding, begging and yanking the pull rope on the engine, it starts every time.

NEVER EAT STINK BAIT

There is no manual to instruct us, just a learned process of precise actions that make our engine the ole reliable machine that it is.

We start with the oil mixture. This is very important. We pour 2-cycle oil into the gas tank with the same precision that Grandma uses when she is cooking—with no recipe. A pinch of this and a dab of that. Gar-Bob pours in some 2 cycle oil, shakes the bottle to scientifically gauge how much is left in it, looks into the portable metal gas tank, glances a questioning gaze at me, and confidently says, "That looks to be 'bout 'nough."

Somedays the smoke trail coming from our exhaust is enough to stop the other boats on the river behind us as they try to peer through our smokescreen. Other days, not so much, and the engine seems to be pinging and starving for a sip of two-cycle oil.

Gar-Bob and I have decided to go fishing today.

When we get to the river boat dock, I back the boat into the river with Gar-Bob sitting proudly in the driver's seat as people respectfully watch us from the bank. The boat dock is a popular spot for people to sit and watch. It is amazing how many people have trouble at the boat dock, and how enjoyable it can be to witness their ineptitude. Not Gar-Bob and me.

With years of experience, I guide the boat and Gar-Bob into the water in a perfectly straight line and out into the river, only to have Gar-Bob go into an imitation of an unhappy coach yelling at a referee from the sidelines, screaming nasty obscenities at me, accompanied with enough arm waving to nearly get him airborne.

The time it takes to let the water drain out of the boat is more than enough for Gar-Bob and me to have a friendly discussion on whose job it was to put in the boat drain plug.

Boat back into the water. Gar-Bob in the boat, his friendly, "I am going fishing smile" gone from his face. I park the pickup. I get into the boat and we begin the starting procedure: Key on—check. Pull the choke lever out—check. Pump up the primer ball—check.

Gar-Bob starts tugging on the pull rope. I push in the choke, pull out the choke. Gar-Bob is beginning to pant as he continues to pull on the start rope. I am multitasking—manning the choke and pumping the worn-out primer ball, trying to propel gas to the engine. I hold the five-gallon gas tank up in the air with the engineering idea of gravity helping us in this task of delivering gas to the carburetor.

Gar-Bob tries to talk between gasping for air, "You flooded it, don't you know how to start the engine?"

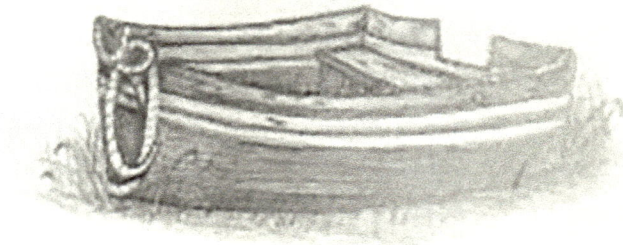

NEVER EAT STINK BAIT

We regroup. Get our breath. Make a few comments on each other's ancestry and accumulation of personal knowledge.

Next on the starting procedure check list is to pull the spark plug and use Gar-Bob's lighter to heat it. We reinstall the heated plug back into the engine. A single gentle pull on the rope and the engine roars to life, or at least it is sputtering along.

With his hand on the tiller—our boat is not one of those rich man's boats with a steering wheel—Gar-Bob clunks the engine into reverse. We have to wait a short time until the excessive cloud of blue smoke clears out, so we can see where we are going.

"Got 'nough oil inh'r today, didn't we," Gar-Bob proudly reports.

Between coughs I reply, "Yep."

"The ole girl started pretty easy today," Gar-Bob declares as he wipes the sweat from his forehead.

I notice the people on the bank loading up their folding chairs and heading out. I guess they do not think there is going to be anybody else to watch and laugh at today.

Bad days of boating experience have taught Gar-Bob and me to always go upstream first. If we have a boating problem, we can always float back to the dock. But if our engine does not run, it is a lot harder to swim upstream against the current. I am not ready to do a Lewis and Clark reenactment.

Gar-Bob was never too good at math, so things like weight-to-power ratios do not mean much to him. Gar-Bob has enough gear stowed away in the boat to supply the entire Lewis and Clark expedition and their two-year journey.

Our little three-bladed, 35-horse power prop is struggling against the current of the Mighty Mo to propel us upstream. Full steam, engine trimmed up and going top RPM, with this much weight, the boat will go around sixteen miles per hour. But the river current is going about seven miles per hour, so we are traveling about nine miles of blazing speed per hour up river. Just enough to keep ahead of Lewis and Clark and their non-engine-powered boats.

It is evening and the water is still and smooth, the boat skimming across the surface, barely leaving a wake to mark that we have been here. Cool evening air is in my face. If there were porpoises jumping in the water alongside us, it would be like we were sailing off Nantucket in our yacht.

The only discord in our trip upstream was the occasional cough in the engine. "I think there is a l'ttle water in the gas," Gar-Bob states.

I am sitting in the front of the boat and do not even bother to turn around to make a sarcastic remark about how twenty minutes ago the gas tank was floating in a boat full of water. This would only renew the dialog about Gar-Bob not admitting he forgot to put in the drain plug.

Gar-Bob and I are going to go catfishing tonight. We get to a likely spot behind a wing dike and tie up. Our plan is to fish until about midnight and then head back to the boat dock with our expected load of freshly caught fish.

A few hours into our wait, it becomes obvious that the catfish are not aware of our plan. No fish in the boat, not even a nibble. Now, Gar-Bob and I have weathered many fishless fishing trips, but the mosquitoes were quite persistent tonight.

NEVER EAT STINK BAIT

"I can get rid of the sqe'ters. All I have to do is let the engine run for af'w minutes and they will be dead and gone," Gar-Bob boasted.

Even though the thought of being rid of those pesky critters sounded good, the engine running would ensure the fish would be discouraged to come our way.

I say out loud something that goes against the grain of any fisherman—"We could go home early."

"What, and leave when they are about to start biting?" Gar-Bob says as he swats at a mosquito sucking blood out of his arm. "Ok," he says.

In no time at all, we have reeled in our lines, untied the boat and are off heading down stream. It is a moonless night and pitch black out, but even in the black of the night, I know that behind us are millions of dead mosquitoes that have suffocated in the smoky, oil-tainted air.

Moving again was a relief from the last couple of hours of having my body and blood being used as a stationary target.

The engine is running smoothly now. Going with the current, we are running full power. At this speed, we will be at the boat dock in no time.

Suddenly the engine lets out a couple of snorts, begins a short period of decline and then dies. The quiet of the night engulfs us.

I don't bother to turn around. I know that sound. The first gas tank has run dry. I sit patiently as I hear Gar-Bob begin to move around. The familiar clanking as Gar-Bob unhooks the primary gas tank and couples the gas hose to the secondary gas tank. But soon the noises quit. It is back to eerie silence.

BRYAN MELLAGE

I turn my flashlight on and look back toward Gar-Bob. Gar-Bob is leaning back against the Evinrude, cigarette in his mouth, as tranquil as a trophy buck deer the day after rifle season has closed. He is sitting there, looking like a man without a care in the world. The calmness of a person who does not have a debt to his name, which I know is not the truth. The only noise is the water as it slides along the side of the boat.

Gar-Bob is a good fishing buddy and would do anything to help me, but he is not one to overdo anything. His demeanor is one of, "Tomorrow would be a good day to do that." Calling Gar-Bob lazy would just be mean—he has a relaxed way about him.

A sense of urgency came through my voice as I said, "Hook up the other gas tank and get the engine started so we don't float to somewhere we shouldn't."

Gar-Bob takes a slow, easy, deep, peaceful drag on his cigarette. His long, extended exhale resembles a yoga exercise as he tries to cleanse himself of all the bad things going on in his life. The red glow of the cigarette tip illuminates his face as he answers me, "Why, ther' ain't no gas in it."

Ensuing was a minor debate, again, about our mothers' lineages and whose turn it was to fill the spare gas tank with petrol.

A quick flashlight inspection of the boat proved there were no oars within the confines of our vessel. Another conference about life in general and that if we had an oar, whose head it likely would end up against.

After all the words had been spoken, we sit in the boat, silent. The darkness of the night is replaced by the gloom of

NEVER EAT STINK BAIT

black despair. The only lighted break in the visionless abyss is when Gar-Bob takes another intense drag from his firestick.

I give up and begin to use my hands to work our way to the Nebraska side of the river. I do not want to go to Iowa or Missouri tonight, not that I am that contrary to those states and that side of the river; our wagon is on the Nebraska side.

Wish I had one of Lewis and Clark's oars about now. Bet ole Lewis is watching and laughing to himself on how he knew that newfangled engine would break down and leave us high and floating down the river.

Prefish

*P*refiks is the root of *prefix*.

I know that you did not come here for an English lesson; otherwise you would have already moved to the back of the room and put your sunglasses on, so please try and stay conscious, or I will be obligated to wake you with my yard stick.

Prefix means, "A word joined to another word to alter or create a new word."

A new word, like say—prefish. So what is "prefish?" Well, *pre* means, "In front of or before."

And, of course, we know what fish is. To fish: to relax, enjoy, lounge, unstress (another new word), exit the rat race for a while, and let the world go by.

So, it only goes to say that prefish would mean, "What happens in front of, or at the beginning of, fishing." Well, my reasoning is: The only thing I want to do more than fishing, is to get ready to go fishing. Prefishing sounds like the second best thing a man could possibly be doing.

The problem with the English language is that many words can have dual meanings. Take "duck" for instance. When I hear the word duck, I think of *quack quack*. But duck can also mean "to duck." Like what I should have done when Gar-Bob and one of my so-called friends, B-Nut, snuck up behind me, and chucked a dead creek chub at me. Usually , "to duck" only works if someone forewarns you to do so. Needless to say, I had to wipe the fish slime off my bald head before we could go inside.

The same thing is true for "cookie." I hear cookie, and my mind wanders off to Grandma's house and the smell of freshly-baked chocolate chip cookies. But "cookie" can also have a meaning only understood by social-media-maniacal, nerdistic (another new word), internet-savvy 12-year-olds.

Apparently it has something to do with why my computer does not work after I have been wading in the internet (I do not surf). Get your mind out of the gutter. I was looking for a birthday gift for my wife. Something normal, like sexy underbritches with "Take me fishing" printed on them. She has going to love them.

"Fall" is another word that can be misleading. Fall is a wonderful time of year. The Great Outdoors is transformed into an artist's paint well. It is truly a banquet for the eyes, as all the colors of the rainbow are strewn out on nature's canvas. Fall is one of the great worldly gifts we humans are able to enjoy. But "fall" can also suggest one too many tequilas at Gar-Bob's birthday party. More appropriately stated, "I have fallen and I can't get up."

Yes, words themselves can give a person a false sense of understanding, and words and phrases can be interpreted differently by different people.

The simple word "boss," for example.

The meaning of "boss" can be different depending on which side of the fence you are standing on at the time. The CEO of a company might feel himself the boss to his loyal, satisfied employees. He smiles to himself in the mirror, knowing that he is the leader, the sage, the cream of the crop, and the brains of the operation. But stand at the time-clock in the morning as the company's dedicated workforce shuffles by with their eyes barely open, shoulders slouched, and dragging their feet, and "boss" may take on a different meaning. To those punching the clock, the boss is "The Man." If he were to ask this sullen group of minions what boss means, he might hear: The jerk in charge, the person who takes credit for all the good ideas, the man with the whip, and other descriptions that would be laced with most of the four-letter words in the Anglo-Saxon language.

A similar grammar anomaly happened when I was a teenager and Dad asked me about my latest grade in algebra. I told him, "I'm doing fine, Dad."

What I did not know was that the teacher had sent my report card to my mom and dad. My teacher seemed to believe differently and had a much-altered opinion of my math skills. My thought was, a D- meant that I had not flunked; but the teacher's interpretation was that I was a seed of a flower waiting to bloom. I never did blossom into the next Einstein, but I did learn to make sure I always checked the mailbox at report card time before my parents got there. You had two (three, but mom and dad count as one here) people with two separate variants of thought for the same letter of the alphabet.

I watched this twist of language play out in front of my eyes one day at the doctor's office. I was in line to get checked in. Funny how the rusty tip of a 6/0 circle hook broken off under your fingernail can fester up like that. The woman ahead of me had weathered her years quite well. Even though modern medicine had given her the look of a woman years younger, her senior-citizen discount was obviously already in place. The attendant, with her head down, asked this attractive older woman how many years she has lived upon this Earth. The attendant quickly looked up, no doubt awakened by the holes being burned in her head from the laser beams directed at her from this woman's eye sockets. This woman—let's call her my mom—pulled herself up to her full height, pulled her wrinkles taut, and with the grace of a queen said, "I am 59, thank you for asking."

Now, given my age, even my rudimentary math skills knew this equation could not work. Yet, this is more proof that a question, or statement, or phrases as well as many words in the English language can—and many times will—have diverse connotations.

So, with our English lesson complete and the awareness that words and phrases can have different meanings depending on the person and situation, let's take this new-found knowledge out for a walk.

If I call my brother-in-law Gar-Bob and say, "Come on over to the garage and we will prefish." Instantly my senses are alive with the sounds, smells, and memory flashes of cold beer, stink bait and retelling of lies—I mean stories—of the big ones that got away. Prefish conjures up a vision of hours of constructive chores such as tying on hooks, relining of reels, and melting down of lead sewer pipe to make weights— now that has to be a brain builder. Prefish gives the notion of a dedication to the sport of fishing—that I am willing to take time out of my busy schedule to get ready to go fishing.

Just mentioning the word *prefish* is like the dawning of a new day, the awakening of nature in the spring, the promise of a new year; it foretells of great things to come.

I get shivers of excitement running through my entire body just thinking about prefishing. It is the simple, but essential, act and actions of, planning of, thinking of, talking of, and getting ready for fishing.

But to another person, prefishing might not have the same implication. When my wife hears me softly say the enticing, erotic, intoxicating word *prefish*, she also gets excited, but not for the same reason.

To her, *prefish* has a whole different set of definitions. To her, prefish means "What happens in front of, or at the beginning of, fishing." This includes such activities as rearranging the attic, trimming the hedges, fertilizing the yard, cleaning out the gutters, washing the car, painting the shed, fixing the back door hinge, replacing all the burned-out light bulbs, replacing the brakes on the car and all the other deeds needing to be done BEFORE I can go fishing.

So, I have learned another lesson. I am still planning on, and I will continue to, *prefish*. So there is no confusion with what meaning we are going to use—I think I am going to sneak out the back door and prefish over at Gar-Bob's fish shack.

That Stinks Good

Ever make a mistake? Well, it happens to the best of us.

After an outdoor cookout get-together at our house, we cleaned up all the leftovers and threw them in the trash can under the sink. Out of sight, out of mind.

Done deal.

The next day we were set to head out on a family camping trip. It was warm summer day; as a matter of fact, the asphalt was melting. Since we were going to be gone for two whole days, I shut off the house AC—frugal man that I am. We arrived back home late and tired, and we hit the pillows.

The next morning was trash day. I pulled open the cabinet door, and the odor of that trash can had a smell that said it could be catfish bait—TODAY!

Speaking of catfish bait.

No matter how many double-dog dares you get, under no circumstances should you EVER poke your finger into the catfish bait bucket and pluck out a finger load and pop it into your mouth.

I have those kinds of friends who will nip at your heels, just looking for any signs of weakness. Their use of that dare thrown at my feet was like the rustling sound of someone opening a new sack of potato chips—I could not help myself.

Once I made the mistake of putting the catfish bait in my mouth, the first thing I thought was, "Golly gee, it didn't smell that bad."

And if you believe I thought, "Golly gee," then I have some prime real estate in the flood zone along the river I would like to sell you.

All my bodily functions went on autopilot. I have only lived through this kind of total stomach upheaval one other time.

As a younger man, standing in a picturesque Wyoming High Plains hayfield one brisk early morning, a fellow worker offered me a wad of "tobaace."

Well, I surmised, I am a man, I am wearing a cowboy hat, I can do this. So, a little between my cheek and gum.

Lickity-split, I lost the ability to stand erect. On my hands and knees, as I contemplated my life, I became aware that the sun and moon seemed to be coming up over the horizon and setting down behind that far mountain, again and again. It was then that it dawned on me that the world was revolving around and around and around and around—quite quickly. Even though it was only a few degrees above zero, the sweat was flowing from my forehead as if I were in a Roman sauna. My mouth was open and saliva was running out of my mouth, along with most everything else that had been in my digestive tract from the last month. My stomach cramped so hard that I am sure my belly button touched my spine. I was afraid it would never pop back out.

Eventually I did recover, a mite older and a great deal wiser.

Even as bad as my first, and last, encounter with "tobaace" was, it did not get me ready for the day I succumbed to the challenge laid down by my so-called friends.

Once that catfish bait was within the confines of my mouth, my brain immediately sent out the ejection signal. But I could not risk losing my manhood status in front of these demented folks whom a few moments ago I considered my friends. The same people who now were on the ground laughing so hard they hurt themselves.

The next intelligent thought (this from a person who has taken up eating catfish bait as a pastime) that came from my simple brain was to swallow this ball of foul-tasting hors d'oeuvre as fast as I could, so it would be past the taste buds.

Even after several beers, and I do mean several, the taste was still there. It lingered until the next page on the calendar had been turned.

Catfish bait is a magical substance that contains enough stench and vulgar taste to make a buzzard go away hungry.

If smell is all that it takes to catch a catfish, I think I am going to put my brother-in-law's socks on a hook and throw them in the creek. I should have a stringer full of catfish in no time. Besides, we have been looking for a place to put his socks.

I spent my summers growing up at my grandpa and grandma's house. They raised chickens, and once, after a morning of butchering chickens, my grandpa did something that raised the question of my grandpa's cerebral wellbeing.

He took a large supply of chicken entrails and placed them in a Ball jar. For you youngsters, that is a canning jar that you put vegetables in. This is what people did before they invented supermarkets. He then put that jar full of large and small chicken intestines out in direct view of the sun.

Now, I was still a person with limited years under my belt, but I did understand the effect of the sun's power and knew what was going to happen to the contents of that jar.

I did not ask why. I just put it in the category of things I had yet to comprehend.

Couple of days later, Grandpa said, "Let's go fishing!" Fishing with Grandpa was the best. It was what great days were made of. We loaded the fishing gear and then Grandpa said, "Go get the jar."

What? The jar? Why would we need the jar? Was Grandpa scared we would be accosted by thieves and need to defend ourselves? Throwing the jar at them and releasing what was in the jar would surely send them backpedaling.

I did as I was told.

After we got to the creek, we got all our equipment out, and then Grandpa reached for the jar of ex-chicken parts.

When Grandpa opened up that jar, the smell of those fermented chicken guts crawled out of the jar, floated across the atmosphere, reached up, and slapped me across the face.

NEVER EAT STINK BAIT

Then to my astonishment, Grandpa reached in the jar, got a hold of some of it, and held it out to me and said, "Here, put some on your hook."

Are you kidding? I know my grandpa. He believed, as we all should, that the wildlife around us is a gift, and anything you shoot or catch is not something to be wasted—but to be taken home and eaten.

I did not want to put into my mouth anything that had eaten those stinking chicken guts.

Catfish bait technology has risen to the heights of highly contested battles of who can concoct the most offensive-smelling, gooey substance for the business of catching catfish.

For unless it stings your nasal cavity just to smell it, makes your nostrils flare and your eyes water, it is not worth the time it takes to put it on the hook.

You will know when you are witness to good catfish bait.

One drizzly cloudy day, I walked into Gar-Bob's ole fishing shack, and before I could adjust my senses to the smells of the surroundings, I had a jar rammed up under my nose.

Gar-Bob said, "Wh't ya think? I just made up a new batch of catfish bait. My best recipe yet!"

The river rat friends I run around with are constantly rushing up to me, presenting me with strange looking containers and saying, "Smell this." I can only offer one bit of advice to you—DON'T.

As my eyes squinted and I was rubbing my nose with my shirt sleeve, I began to cough and gag at the same time. In between stomach spasms and trying to hold down my noon hash, I uttered, "That stinks good."

Lost in an Illusion

A man's house is his castle. That is the way it is at my house. I do not need a man cave; the whole house is my cave. This is my house. I am the undisputed leader of this abode. What I say goes without question.

How could there be any disputes about that statement? I own all the guns in the gun safe. The hunting dog out in the pen only answers to me. The boat in the shed has my name on the title. All the fishing tackle lumped in the garage is mine. I drive a pickup, wear boots and have calluses on my hands. I have worked hard to become the leader in my domain. All the residents in this household have deep respect for my wishes and commands.

I am in complete control.

When I drive into the driveway at night, the dog jumps to his feet, my Redheaded wife and the obedient children stand at the back door waiting for me to enter and give me a welcome home kiss and reverent hug. They help take off my shoes and offer me an "after-a-hard-day-at-work drink."

It is good to be king.

Like I said—"I am lost in an illusion."

I am not sure how it happened. I went into marriage with my eyes open. I thought I knew what was going to happen. I am not exactly sure when the fog began to rise from around my feet to engulf me in a cloudy gray existence, but it has.

But the longer the wife and I have been married, the vaguer the governance over my realm has become. There has even been recent discussion over our wedding vows. Although I distinctly remember her saying the word, "Obey" as part of the wording, she refuses to acknowledge that it happened that way.

One night, not all that long after we had gotten married and she had vowed blessed obedience to me, I was relaxing on the throne in the living room. The smile on my face showed contentment in the knowledge of my power over all that I could see.

In the kitchen my dutiful wife was working to bring to me the evening meal. The kitchen had been the scene of a "mild" argument just the night before. It surprised me to learn that one of the subjects in my kingdom was unhappy with the situation.

The wife wanted a microwave. Now, my grandmother did not have one, my mother did not have one, and they both had cooked all the meals in their house. So I said, "NO. You do not need a microwave and we will never have one." I laid down the law. That was that.

As I sat in my chair of power, still fully in belief of my total dominance, the doorbell rang. I opened the door to find a friend of mine holding a microwave and he asked, "Where do you want it?"

My wife sprinted out of nowhere and helped guide him to the kitchen where she had already cleaned off a spot for it on the counter. I was still standing at the entryway, holding the door. I was scared to move because I could not see for the fog. We still have that microwave today.

As the smoke of the illusion continued, I was even more confused. I could tell the wife I was going to go hunting or fishing and she did not even raise an eyebrow. She seeminglyalmost encouraged me to leave the castle.

One splendid sunny day I left the cave for the forest to perform my manly hunting and foraging duties, and upon returning I wandered too far into the house. There was a trail of muddy footprints leading from the back door right to where I was standing. Even the king knows better than to muck up the carpet.

One of the kids said, "I'll go get the vacuum cleaner." Now, I knew that the vacuum was on the fritz. I had told the wife that we did not need to buy a new one. I was going to repair the old one, and even though it had only been a few short months, I had assured her that I was going to get that done. Sure enough, our eldest son came dashing around the corner, busting through the murky cloud like Belushi and the Deathmobile did heading for the grandstand, with a bright, shiny, new vacuum cleaner.

The vapor emitting from my lost world continued to rise and surround me. The Redhead materialized as a wizard from the haze and said, "Thank you for the Christmas present." The shadowy atmosphere I stood engulfed in prohibited the family seeing me there, frozen in place, mouth open and my eyes blinking in total disbelief of what had just happened.

In the early days of home cinema entertainment, we had something that I am sure Generation Y has never heard of—video cassettes. So new and revolutionary was this technological marvel that no one owned their own VCR player. You would rent not only the movie you wanted to watch for the weekend, but the VCR player as well.

So it goes, our family huddled around the boob tube one Saturday night, popcorn in hand, to watch one of Disney's best on the rented hi-tech contraption. During the movie, the lovely affectionate wife snuggles up to me and seductively whispers, "We should buy one of these for our very own."

"Are you kidding?" I said, "These things are a flash in the pan. A year from now they will be just a memory, and we will go back to watching the good ole three TV stations that have served us so well. NO, we do not need a VCR player."

She understood that the law had been laid down and the subject was not broached again. I felt the power of a governor just pardoning an execution. My chest puffed out and I slept that night refreshed in the glow of my supremacy.

Sunday evening came around and we were again watching the same movie. You were only allowed to rent one. The wife smiled and said that she did not have time that day to return the player and would do it the next day.

I walked into the house Monday evening, after my hard manly day of breaking boulders and could hear the sound of children laughing and the TV. The three stations of old would only have news programs on right now. I knew something was afoot as the kids were too young yet to see the humor in the news. I looked into the TV room to see the same movie playing again. I stomped into the kitchen where I began to

NEVER EAT STINK BAIT

"teach" the wife about high finance. If we kept renting that tech-fangled thing, we would end up buying it.

Suddenly, I had to use my arms and hands to swipe the smog from around my head, and I lost sight of the Redhead. It was as though my ole, in need of a tune-up pickup's tailpipe was sticking through the window. I had to feel my way through the house because of the endless billowing clouds of lost control.

Only when I stepped outside did I re-enter a world of clear vision. I went to the wood pile and split firewood. Nobody seemed to bother me out here.

I once walked erect; my stride showed purpose and my life was lived in a world of black and white. The unwritten rules of the household were clear and my role as leader of the tribe was accepted as fact. Standing in the middle of the house I could simply raise my hand and those around me would stop their activities and with faithful attention wait for my next decree or bit of spoken wisdom.

Ever since the flood of murkiness had floated into the palace, things had taken a turn for the surreal. Or, better described as a change of management.

Nowadays I sit, like Eeyore, with a cloud over my head, in my chair. The title of throne has been removed. The old chair is thread-worn, stuffing sticking out of the edges. It leans to one side, and no longer will it recline, nor does eminence radiate from it. I sit in it, listening to the TV. I cannot see the picture for the fog.

Old kings do not die; they just fade away into the mist.

BRYAN MELLAGE

fisherman's wife

To make the grade and become a fisherman's wife is no easy task. It probably should be an Olympic sport. The skills for this career are not taught in the curriculum of a basic high school home economics class. Martha Stewart does not provide the training needed for the "girl next door" to be ready for the onslaught of having a fisherman as a lifelong housemate.

Quality parenting requires a daughter's mother to inform her daughter about the trials and tribulations that will be hers if she chooses a fisherman as a husband. Fathers cannot hold back their distain when they see the boyfriend pull up to pick up their little baby girl in a muddy old beat-up pickup truck with a bunch of fishing poles sticking out of the broken-out back window.

For that reason, I would like to help all you young fishermen. There will be a time when you will want to throw your hook toward something other than a five-pound large-mouth bass.

I know that you do not believe me now, but it will happen.

As I myself approached manhood, I had become very skilled in knowing what kind of lure to use on a cloudy day. I could call a turkey right into my blind, and could sneak right up to a big ole buck without his even knowing I was around. But the skills I needed to find the one person who would be willing to wait at home while I spent the day on the lake came hard for me. Here are some tough-learned pointers I have acquired through the education provided to me by the long hard road of what can only be described as "marriage wars."

For starters, if you think (as I did), that marriage is going to be like Jeremiah Johnson, coming back from a hard day scrounging for food to feed the family, strolling up to the little woman who is patiently waiting, (happily) stirring the fire under the scalding pot; and as you meander by, throw in a rabbit, fur and all into the frying pan, while in a strong, manly, husbandly voice say, "Cook this." Let me be the first to tell you that this is not going to happen.

Quickly into my marriage war, I learned to always announce myself. "Hi Honey, I'm home. How was your day?" Then and only then, should you throw the rabbit into the pan.

There are some tried and true passages that do offer some premarital wisdom. One that comes to mind is:

WANTED:

Good woman, likes to fish, and has boat.

Please send picture of boat.

Although this may not be the best way to secure a good woman, let's not misplace this piece of quality wisdom.

One of the ideas that helped me was a prenuptial agreement—a prenup. This is a document where the prospective applicant (my future wife) and I thought about our forthcoming life together, and with the help of one of my buddies at the bar, I wrote it up.

In this document, I tried to think of all the things that would help my future fry cook and me bridge all the so-called trials and tribulations that her parents were so worried about. With everything written down, I surmised it would all be a lot easier for her.

For instance, she would be willing, obligated, happy, and have no qualms about feeding the dog, gutting and cleaning all fish I caught, and preparing any and all game that I brought home, turning it into the evening meal after she got home from her day job.

My marriage scuffle, as with all wars, is not stagnant but is mobile. In our married life, my wife and I have moved several times, and somewhere along the way our prenup, under unknown and very suspicious circumstances, got lost. So here is one of my bits of advice: once you get her to sign the prenup, make a second copy. For without the proof of the prenup, my pretty, red-headed, sometimes-forgetful wife does not remember agreeing to this arrangement.

As I looked for a lifelong partner, I didn't just want someone to clean the house, wash the car, care for the kids, and cook my meals, and neither do you. I wanted a woman who could help me with all those trials and tribulations; I wanted a wife with skills.

Do as I did: Make a list of the talents you are looking for, and on your first date, show her your job-qualification summary. You might want to keep the list to yourself—don't show it to her dad.

A wife should have outdoor abilities such as: How to fillet a bass, bone out a deer, fix a tire, reload shells, remove an embedded fishing hook from your hand, and how to follow a blood trail, as she will be the only one looking for you. After showing your date the list, some young ladies might not understand your straight forwardness. I'm sure her daddy won't. So if she goes back into the house crying, I would release the brake, let the ole pickup start rolling down the hill, drop the clutch, and get out of there.

Maybe of all the talents that make a good wife, cooking should be at the top of the list. I am not talking about heating up a can of beans. I am talking Grandma cooking. A man has to eat. Now, I have known men who could cook and who even do cook. Not me.

Cooking to me is pouring milk on Cheerios. I was lucky on this one. I do not need to find the pot of gold at the end of the rainbow—I get it every night at dinner. My wife can take whatever I bring her—as long as I deskin, defur, descale, debone it, and prepare it to be ready to cook (someday I will find that prenup) and she will turn it into a banquet. She truly knows how to "handle a hungry man."

Go to the local church social or town soup supper and look for a portly fellow with the contented smile of a man at peace with the world, watch what his wife brings to the table, and I will bet you a fishing season of free night crawlers that whatever it is, is good vittles. Use your backwoods expertise to trail them and see if they have a daughter; the rest is up to you. Remember there is a fine line here between trailing and stalking, so you need to blend in. As you birddog them, slouch over, drag your feet and look down at the ground to give the appearance of a defeated man—a married man. All is fair in love and war—and the pursuit of a good woman who can cook.

There is nothing better than the sensation, after a hard day stumbling around in the timber looking for today's calories, of moving the hingeless porch door off to the side, and walking in the house to the aroma of blackened catfish, or tex-mex quesadillas with quail breasts, maybe venison spaghetti or some other scrumptious delight floating through the air.

Your nostrils are full of the smell of tonight's mouthwatering meal when she says the dreaded, "Oh, by the way, the handle broke off the cabinet door—could you fix it before dinner?" Before you know it, you have rehung the door, caulked the shower drain, replaced the hot water heater element, and missed the opening kickoff of tonight's game, and have nothing to look forward to except a small plateful of cold food that is left after the kids and all their friends, who always show up at dinnertime, have had their share.

In the ebb and flow of battle, combatants learn—just as West Point cadets acquire the knowledge of when to attack and when to flank. My "always-way-ahead-of-me wife" has become self-educated in the advanced ways of guerilla tactics warfare.

My little woman has never quit learning, adapting, and coming up with ways to stay ahead of me. I know I will never catch back up.

Obviously, along with all the other wifely skills, I was looking for a good woman to provide me with children because there is no greater thrill in life than sitting on a hard, splinter-infected wooden bleacher in 100 degree heat, watching a tee-ball game while your kid sits on the bench.

But in my wife's defense, she has had to learn how to put up with mud on the back porch deep enough for vegetables to grow in, fish guts in the sink, dead worms in the fridge along with the smell of dead worms in the fridge, being woken up in the middle of the night to be shown the big catch, a load of laundry all stuck together with the treble hooks of a Lazy Ike lure left in the pocket of my shirt, disassembled fishing reels on the dining room table for the duration of the winter, a 10x42 scope for her Valentine's Day present that just happens to fit on my 30-06 and many other so-called trials and tribulations that only a fisherman's wife would understand.

The best thing that the marriage clashes have taught me, which is quite a revelation to my wife's parents to learn that I can be taught, is to make peace. My battle scars are proof enough that my clueless manly education was no match for the strength, determination, and mental capabilities of this red-headed, multi-talented, chef extraordinaire—this fisherman's wife.

I still am amazed that she kisses me goodbye in the morning, although sometimes she seems quite happy that I am leaving. But I'm even more astounded that she is waiting for me by the screenless back door (there seems to be a pattern there) come evening.

My recommendation to all young fishermen: When you see a girl that catches your eye ,ask her if she wants to go fishing. If she says yes, baits her own hook, and invites you back to her place to cook your catch of fish, then give it up. You have lost the battle. Make peace—you have been caught.

Zinger

Have you ever been the recipient of a zinger? I don't mean the delightful-tasting, cream-filled Dolly Madison Zinger that can make any morning go better—I mean zinged.

It was winter, late winter. All my fishing poles and tackle were warm and snugly tucked away, right where I had chucked them at the back of the garage, waiting to be overhauled for next year. Hunting season was over, the Super Bowl score and commercials were but a memory, and there was nothing to do on Saturday night except go to the video store. I was trying to convince my wife, the Redhead, that we could have a dreamy, night-out-on-the-town date—going to the store to rent a movie. Even though she was a bit skeptical, the little woman and I were soon cruising through the aisles of cinema-boxed experiences. My lovely bride, the person whom I have decided to spend the rest of my days with, holds out a choice from the "How To" selection area and says, "Maybe you should get this video on how to catch a fish!"

Zing! Ouch, direct hit. Boy did that hurt!

My body is decorated top to bottom with the scars of past zingers.

Zingers are like laser beams and once emitted, look for a target. Zingers can also bounce or glance off objects. Just like Ralphie's worst nightmare of his official Red Ryder Carbine-Action Two Hundred Shot Range Model Air Rifle's BB pellet ricocheting back and "shooting his eye out," my zingers have a tendency to rebound back and smack me right between the eyes.

I have been told that some people are born salesmen, a business owner or even destined to be a politician, although I would wish that on no one. Myself, I do not believe that there are any predetermined status or personality traits for us. Most of us use life experiences to give us our demeanor, outlook on and vocation in life. However, the wife and I did have one child who seemed to hit the ground with a preconceived notion that green was no good. The only way we could get him to eat green beans was to paint them orange. But there are those who seem to be born with the ability to zing. It just comes natural to them.

I myself am not one of those lucky ones. I want to zing, but have a zing block. I am zing-impaired. For those who are naturally zing-ready, they seem to be able to respond with a properly placed zing no matter the situation. These Zingers can even bundle zings and throw zing bombs on whole crowds of unsuspecting Zingees. To be a zingfaso, you should be quick and witty. The fact that I am slow and dull may give an indication as to why I have not graduated from zing school.

I have to surrender to the fact that I am zing-challenged, destined to be a lifelong zing want-to-be. When the situation arises for me to utter my zing, I am speechless. I stand there with my mouth open, drops of drool dripping from the corners of my lips, my feeble brain a complete blank, my eyes with that unable-to-blink stare and my face frozen in a look of—DUH. In my zing conundrum, my mind searches through all the stored information of zing comebacks it has, but the synapses just don't connect and I have to just walk away, zingless.

Later, usually in the middle of the night, I awake to the core of my zing troubles. I now have the zing. I know what to say. It is 3:00 in the morning, and I contemplate calling the person to deliver the zing. I know that it will not have the same effect that it would have had twelve hours ago, but I also know that by morning, I will not remember the zing, and it will have floated off to the zing abyss and be gone forever.

Some can even zing from afar. A hunting buddy of mine and I set up a date to go pheasant hunting together. I anticipated a day that would be spent in the field chasing Mr. Roo with an old high school companion who was also a very close friend. He had recently moved to the jungle of metal and cement in the big capital city of Lincoln. Being the hick small-town boy that I am, anytime I go to a city with more than one stop light, I need directions. My "buddy" gave me the driving instructions to his house the night before.

This was several decades before Global Positioning. Growing up without the luxury of knowing where I was at any given moment never was an issue with me or my friends. Matter of fact, looking back, it was something of a blessing in

BRYAN MELLAGE

disguise. The kids today get a block away from the back door and they need the help of satellites to guide them.

As a young lad, I had issues getting out of bed and heading off to school, but on Saturday mornings, I was out the back door at full gallop. My friends and I would spend the whole day floating down the creek, wallowing in any mud we could find, chasing butterflies in the pastures—literally lost in nature. But every late afternoon, as the sun began to approach the horizon, which seemed to correspond with suppertime, I would miraculously find my way to the back door of the house, never once looking at my hand-held device for help.

Plan was, my "buddy" and I were going to go out mid-morning and catch the wily roosters after their mid-morning brunch out in the grain fields and were back in the cover of heavy grass. I drove into the big city during the morning rush hour traffic, and I was as scared as the chicken trying to get to the other side of the road. I had my "buddy's" driving instructions on the seat beside me. I was driving and reading my non-electronic paper map. I took a left by the big tree, a right by the old building that looked like my uncle's old barn, several more turns, stop signs and lights, one after another. Lewis and Clark did not have this much trouble. Just one more right and I would be there. I looked down at my handwritten GPS road map to make sure I was doing it correctly, and when I looked back up, there was a herd of morning commuters coming right at me. Three lanes of honking, finger-waving, extremely unhappy, over-caffeinated 8 to 5'ers heading west as I looked into the sun. ZING!

When I got to my bBuddy's" place, he was sore from laughing. He said that he did not get a wink of sleep last night just thinking about me turning into the one way street during morning traffic. The rest of the day walking the grass, my "buddy" was yelling out "Turn Left"—"Turn Right" and directions for me on which way to go. Quietly, in my mind, I was thinking of places he could go.

The life of those of us who bear the brunt of the zings can be hard.

Of course, just because you can zing doesn't mean you should zing. There can be long lasting repercussions. The wife and I were walking down the aisle of the grocery store, on another one of our romantic nights out, when I noticed the book stand, and without even thinking about the fallout said, "Hey Honey, here is a cookbook you should buy." Ricochet and thud, another zing pock mark right between the eyes.

Cold cereal and baloney sandwiches for a month.

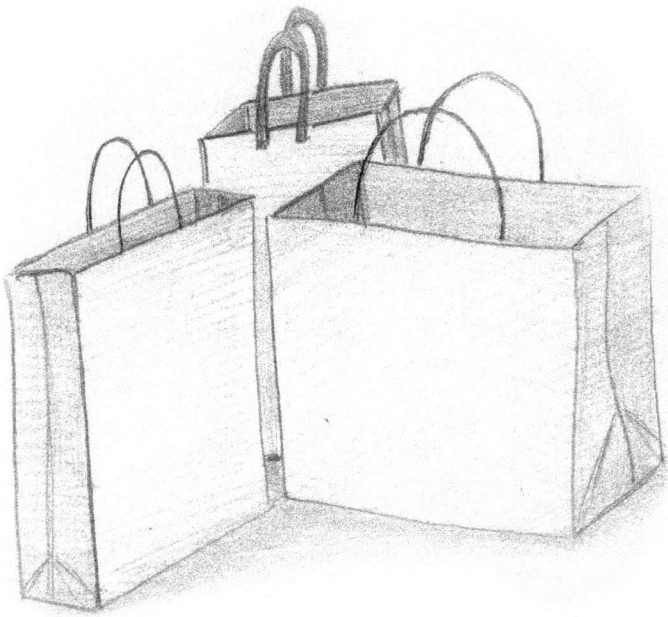

Christmas shopping, Medieval Tortures & Other Indignities

I gazed out the window, downhearted.

It had been warm and dry all week. No trackable snow, zero humidity, no moisture of any kind in the grass to help the dog track the scent of Mr. Pheasant. There was not even a slight breeze that would allow me to sneak up on the birds from downwind. Maybe I would not go bird hunting today.

Just the thought seemed shocking and strangely... strange.

The sun comes up every morning. I reach my cell phone in the other room immediately after it quits ringing. One of the kids throws up all over the back seat on the family vacation. And I go bird hunting every weekend I am able during pheasant season.

There is another alarming issue that is painful to even think about—pain. Who knew that this Herculean, muscle-toned body that I have lived in for these fifty-plus went-by-way-too-fast years would get nicks, rips, and worn pieces and parts. I vividly remember, in my indestructible, "I'll-never-grow-old" youth being told by my grandfather, "Just wait, your time will come."

Time for what? Riches and glory? Accolades and acknowledgments? What was he talking about? Who knew? Boy, did I not know.

Now I have arrived at the point in my life that I am standing in the grocery store checkout line being asked by the baby-faced, not-a-clue-about-life child clerk for my senior discount card. I now see life from a different vantage point.

My whole body aches, all my joints creak like rusty hinges, and my knees just plain hurt. A player in the NFL with a sports injury lounging in his easy chair, thinking about catching the game-winning touchdown pass, can, with that thought (and glancing at his checkbook balance), console himself.

Trying to get comfortable on the couch with throbbing knees as a reward for a day out stumbling through fields of dry switchgrass, seeing no birds, I would be very un-consoled, especially with my below-par checkbook numbers.

Then the Redhead utters the unspeakable: "You could go with your sister and me—Christmas shopping."

Truth be known, I was the one who actually brought up this mind-boggling notion—but some of the words have been changed to protect the innocent.

So I traded hunting boots, shotgun shells and the goose bump feeling of the dog-on-point to what I knew was going to be a drab, dull day of just going shopping for trinkets and gifts. An easy day, with no painful physical repercussions.

The look on my dog's face as we pulled out of the driveway showed he could not comprehend what was going on. I felt like a police car prisoner in the back seat (not that I have been there—for a long time) as we headed to the land of a Santa in every store and the cement jungle of the big city.

I sat there in the back seat alone, a little fearful and apprehensive of what I had gotten myself into.

A chocolate treat came sailing toward me from the front seat.

My sister said, "If you are good, stay quiet, and don't whine, we'll give you another one later."

Now I know how my dog must have felt when I trained him as a puppy.

My first mistake on the adventure came when I asked what the plan was.

"What plan?" was the reply.

They didn't have a plan? How could this be? They didn't know what store they were going to first, or when they were going to stop for dinner and a beer? They did not have a single strategic blueprint of any kind for their assault of gift procurement?

My sister said, "Our only requirement is that we have to be home on the same calendar day we left. There are no other rules or plans."

My mind went into freefall.

We came to a stop at our first location. Both my wife and my sister turned and fixed their scorching stare onto me. It was time for the pep talk.

They verbally attacked from all sides, like a coach before the playoff game, with pieces of sagely advice and shopping wisdom.

"Stay hydrated."

"Try to keep up."

"Show no fear."

"Tie your shoe strings tight."

"Stay focused."

From one store to the next we went. Then back to the car and off to the next spot on our treasure hunt. The drive between each store illuminated the leading-edge team my sister and wife had become. If shopping were an Olympic team sport, this was a gold-medal squad.

They worked together like my hunting partner and I, as spotter and blocker, on a pheasant hunt drive. My sister blared out commands and pointed to open spots in the traffic ahead of us and my wife would dart the car into spots not big enough for the length of the vehicle. Only the speed and daring of her shopping skills kept us from being hooked up to and dangling from a tow truck. We ducked in and out of several stores, each time exiting with wrapped riches specially chosen for a particular family member.

Years of hunting our home area's countryside has allowed my hunting partner and me an in-depth knowledge of where to go and how to best hunt these haunts. The shopping duo in the front seat rivaled anything I had ever seen or was capable of. They knew where to go, which door to enter to be closer to the particular spot they wanted to reach first, and where everything was in every store. This twosome worked together as a cohesive team. They were on a next-level playing field from the other mall riff raff. All the others were just shopper want-to-bes not capable of keeping up with the shadow of these two, discount coupons in hand—super shoppers.

I then made my next blunder and blurted out, "Are we about done?" A piece of chocolate came flying from the front seat as we pulled up to an area different from all the other landscapes they had shown me so far. There were buildings as far as I could see. The ground itself moved with the hustle and bustle of Christmas activity.

My sister informed me, "Those other stores were just pre-game—we haven't even started yet. We are at the mall and now it's about to get real."

The car doors flung open and in unison they instructed, "Put your game face on, we're going in!"

Instead of birds chirping, wind blowing through the trees, and the gentle sound of the outdoors, now there was only the deafening noise of endless Christmas songs echoing through the halls of the mall. Only the great animal migrations on the plains of the Serengeti rival the elbow gouging, pushing, and shoving mass of faceless shopping zombies I witnessed. Far off in the distance, the yelp of a coyote hadbeen replaced with a youngster having a melt down and making sure his parents and all within hearing distance knew of his displeasure.

I dropped into the jet stream of my shopping mentors and fell into the abyss of endless consumerism. I had lost any of my own shopping mastery and had tumbled into mindless roaming mode. I looked around and felt the stark, scared fear of being lost in the wilderness. No sun in the sky or familiar markings to enable me to get my bearings.

Then from above the din of the crowd came a voice I knew. Like a young penguin in the vast penguin village hearing his mother's voice, my ears strained to hear, "Walk faster, keep up!" A piece of chocolate hit me in the forehead.

I was surprised to find splotches of shrubbery and grasslands in the open areas between the never-ending structures of shops. I did my best to find signs or footprints of wildlife within these scattered patches of urban backwoods. Maybe some deer tracks, or a lost pheasant—anything to make me believe there were still some holdouts of animal life. Even a bunny would have been a welcome discovery.

Then a voice. "Hey, what are you doing in there?" The landscaping man was not pleased with my exploration of his manicured ground cover, which was obvious by the way he was shaking his tree shears at me.

At last, the three of us burst out of the double doors to freedom and broke the grip this macabre mall had on us and began our return journey across the parking lot. You can spin me, drop me blindfolded on a cloudy day in the middle of a vast trackless backwoods, and I can pinpoint north and make my way to civilization. But, I was still in shopping-mall mode and could not find my way.

I would have not been able to locate our car if it had a cooler of beer in it. It might have had something to do with the Grinch-sized sledload of presents I was lugging that was blocking my view. I had found my purpose and place on this shopping team and it looked a lot like a pack mule.

The dynamic duo had no such trouble. They walked a straight line toward our sleigh as confident as salmon returning to their birthplace stream. We loaded our hard-fought, earned prizes into the car as the sun began its drop below the city's skyline. It was not the same as a sunset after a satisfying pheasant hunt, but it did signal the end of my first Christmas shopping extravaganza.

We settled in with only a small space left for me in the overstuffed back seat and were on our way home when my sister turned and reported, "You did good, rookie. Maybe next year we'll take you out on Black Friday." Then she handed me the sack of the remaining chocolate treats. The two world-class shoppers exchanged glances and giggles.

After we got home and unloaded all the soon-to-be-under-the-tree Christmas offerings, I fed the dog. He quietly asked me in a muffled tone, "How was it?"

I shook my head and told him, "Just be glad I didn't make you go along." He smiled with understanding and went into his dog house.

Later, as I sat in my easy chair with a drink at my side, I tried my best to get comfortable. My feet hurt, my knees throbbed, I was physically exhausted and mentally drained. I tried to make comparisons to my day out in the world of serious shoppers, unhappy toddlers, and the land of uninterrupted sales and bargains to something familiar I could relate to. What came to mind was my high school history teacher telling us of the medieval days and the torture rooms housed in the basements of ancient castles.

I swallowed a sweet sip of Kentucky's best, along with a strong dose of ibuprofen. Then I reached into the sack of chocolate treats, pop the last one into my mouth, and grin to myself.

Maybe I should take them pheasant hunting?

Nah.

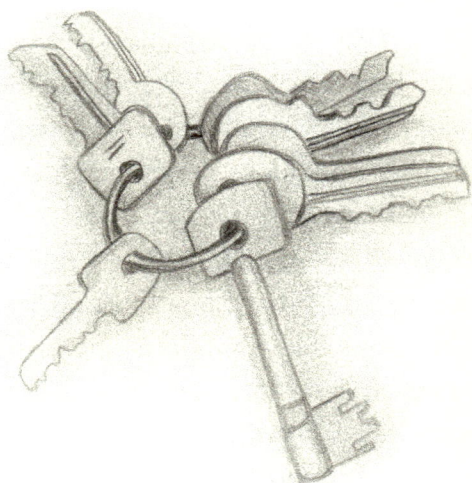

Trapping Ducks

The progression of moving through each of life's steps and the knowledge hopefully learned from them is what living is all about. I was ready for this next stage in my life. Matter of fact, I had been waiting for it all my days, the entire 16 years' worth. This was that glorious day I was to get my driver's license.

I had already taken the written exam—three times. I knew the answers to all the important questions like:

What is the best radio station?

Is it possible to escape detection by driving with your headlights off?

What is the coolest way to hang your elbow out the window?

However, the exam was full of irrelevant questions about braking time, stop signs, turning lanes, and such.

I knew that I was not going to have any trouble with the next part of the ritual. They were not going to issue me a driver's license until they had seen me drive. This was going to be great. After the exhibition I was going to put on, they were not only going to give me my license, but I was also confident of getting pats on the back, a driving medal to hang on the rear view mirror and probably get asked to come back as a celebrity driving instructor. My driving skills would be the material of muffled talks of respect between the test examiners for years to come.

Grandpa had been letting me drive the ole '55 Chevy pickup ever since I could reach the pedals. I could navigate down rough country roads, roar up field waterways and fly over ditches out in the back pasture. Doing a couple easy laps around the courthouse square on flat dry cobblestone would be mere child's play.

The day of the driving exam started out with a suspiciously bad omen. My car, the faithful steed that had been bequeathed to me by my dad lay still in the driveway. No matter how many times I turned the ignition key, beat on the dash or called it names, nothing changed the status of the dead battery. The car had only been mine for a few days, the moment still fresh in my memory.

Dad said, "Walk with me." Out the back door we went, his big, rough, calloused hand firmly on the back of my neck. I was understandably a little nervous, not knowing if Mom had told him about the herd of mice I had shot in the basement of the house with the .22 and birdshot. Who knew we had such strict regulations concerning the discharge of firearms within the household?

Dad guided me over to the old family car. He pointed to it and pronounced, "She's all yours."

I looked up at Dad in disbelief. He didn't know about the mice. I looked at the car and then back at him. Really!? This was better than the time the teacher mistook the homework paper from Donna who sat in front of me, as mine, and I got an A on my Geometry test.

My very own car.

Instantly I saw myself driving through town, elbow casually hanging out the window, music blaring out from the AM radio so staticky I could not understand a single word, and a pretty young lass snuggled up next to me. Dad, seemingly pleased with himself, walked off. As he turned to walk away, I noticed a look on his face, like someone had just told him a joke about a girl spending the night at a farmhouse.

I stared at this bantam box of a car—a faded red two-door Nova. Four bald, flat tires, broken windshield, leaking radiator, exhaust system hanging down all the way to the ground and what I found out later to be a perpetually empty gas tank—yes, this was a wonderful little red dream come true.

So, there I was. Only hours away from showcasing my driving expertise to the world. I had fixed up some of the car's ailments, but I did not have quite enough cash funding to replace the battery yet and now I could not get the car to start.

The solution was easy. I called Grandpa.

"Can I use your car to complete my driving exam?" Grandpa was only too happy to say yes. He answered, "The keys are in it. Come get it."

Since I was not yet in possession of my very own personal driver's license certificate, Mom drove me over to Grandpa's house, and she drove us both to the courthouse in Grandpa's 1974 Ford four-door LTD. Now this was a car built before

Detroit had become aware of things like "miles per gallon" ratings. Mom referred to Grandpa's car as the TANK. In another life, it could have been a very long military-issued armed personnel carrier. Standing at the front bumper and looking down the length of the car, it seemed to go all the way to the horizon.

When we got to the courthouse, Mom parked and asked, "Are you sure you can drive this thing?" I did my best not to give Mom one of those looks that said, "You've got to be kidding me." I assured her that there wasn't anything with wheels that was a match for my well-honed driving skills. She turned and started to walk away and I could have sworn she had the same look on her face as Dad did the day he "gave" me my car.

Later on in my life, Dad finally admitted that the reason he had given me the car was the salvage man had told him that he would not only not take the car, but would charge Dad to even come and get it.

I waited in the car for the instructor to come and administer the test. She was in for an unexpected surprise. After hours on end of testing people who knew nothing about cars, she was about to bear witness to someone who not only had spent his first sixteen years in faithful service beside his Dad at the mechanic shop learning about cars and engines, but had the Mario Andretti car-handling skills to go with it.

She got in and slammed the door behind her. Her cold stare immediately made me blink; my stomach dropped and my mouth went dry. Her name tag said, "Helda." She barked out the command, "Start the car." I looked down at the dash, not remembering where the key was. I was rattled and surprisingly nervous for someone so accomplished at car nomenclature.

She gave a prison-guard growl, and said, "You do know how to drive this car, don't you?"

I could only look back and nod my head up and down—no words would come out.

Well, I got the car started and away we went. Once we were moving, things smoothed out, with only a few mishaps that could happen to anyone. That old guy with the cane jumped out of the way long before I was going to hit him. Then cutting short of a corner in this eighteen-wheeler-long car, I dragged the back tires over the curb with a resounding bump bump, which drew an evil glare from Helda the Hulk.

As we came around the courthouse on the last lap, Helda commanded, "Pull up here and parallel park between these two cars."

I looked straight ahead; arms frozen straight out with my fingers clenched to the steering wheel. Parallel park? Was this a sick joke? Who parallel parks? How can this be a part of the test? The blood began to drain away from my head. I felt faint. I could not muster the strength to chance a look at Helda. I was sure she was wearing the same look she had stolen from my mom and dad.

I threw the gear shift lever up to reverse and tried to herd grandpa's lengthy yacht of a car back into this pint-sized parking slot. I was halfway there. I nosed it as far forward as I dared to go. Now, with my confidence building, reversed again. I allowed the car to creep backwards. I looked into the rearview mirror to no avail, the distance to the back bumper too far to see. Just a little bit more and … Bang!

BRYAN MELLAGE

My head jerked, the car jolted, the clamor of the collision resonated throughout the car, and the echo of the sound seemed to go on forever. I put the car into drive and finished the job of parallel parking.

It had been just a small touch. Maybe Helda did not even notice. I glance her way. I was right. My driving skills had left her speechless. Her mouth was open, teeth were showing and her nostrils were flared. Her glowing red eyes were focused right at my head. She seemed distressed.

I said, "There you go, one parallel-parked car."

Well, the next week I was lucky enough that Helda was elsewhere the day of driving examinations. I had procured a used battery from the salvage yard. I smoothly drove around the courthouse square and without even slowing down stuffed my little red two-door, shorter than the hood of Grandpa's LTD Nova into the parking stall. I walked down the steps of the courthouse that day with a smile on my face and license in hand.

The journey of life is full of next steps. I had acquired a car, procured permission from the state to drive the car and now the next rung in my upward struggle was to figure out how to come up with the money to put fuel in the tank. Funny thing about that. Because fifty years later, I am still trying to locate enough money to put gas in my fuel tank.

When you are sixteen and without management skills, your job choices are limited. You can either sell your integrity, get a job and be a pawn to the boss man telling you what to do next, or you can head to the outskirts of town and run a trap line.

NEVER EAT STINK BAIT

I had friends who had sold out and become slaves of the establishment. Not me. While my friends were inside, protected from the weather, warm and dry, doing whatever the man told them to do, I was up at daybreak, enduring frost-bite-inflicting north winds, and wading waist deep in ice-cold water, checking my traps. Silly them.

A week's worth of furs sold to the local buyer would equate to gas and pizza for the weekend. I soon learned the meaning of the saying, "There is always more weekend at the end of the fur money."

The education of trapping came to good use later in life. When my wife, the Redhead, and I first got married, the income from my trap line was the only thing separating us between our next meal and being hungry. It was that hard first winter and some extreme prodding from the Redhead that made me become part of mainstream thinking—a full-time, go-to-work-every-day job. Like I said—"Life is full of next stages."

Later on when we began to grow our family, the extra money derived from the trap line helped pay for all the extra clothes, food, doctor bills, and other expenses that seem to follow children around.

There was a deep slough that ran north of town. It had a strong spring and would stay open all winter long. This was a gift that kept on giving all winter long. Open water in the middle of winter is a draw that attracts many animals, and most of them were wearing fur.

I had a line of traps along the whole expanse of the watery marsh. I had been running my line for a couple of weeks already. It was Sunday morning and I was getting ready to walk out the back door when I remembered last evening when I was checking the traps I had heard the whistling sound of ducks setting in for the night along the weedy edges of the slough. I tucked the trusty 16-gauge under my arm and headed out to check the trap line.

I was walking along the edge of the water way, half hunched over, not able to stand up for the dense grove of the leafless plum thicket. All of a sudden, the ducks, alerted to my presence, possibly from the cussing and yelling as I plowed my way through the brambles and bushes, took to wing. They got about tree level high. I had just enough of an open spot to bring the gun up and shoot. KA-BOOM. I had winged the duck but it did not fold. He just set his wings and drifted back to the water. When he hit the water, he began to flop and propel himself down the length of the slough. This waterway is quite long and there are a lot of places he would be able to "duck" in and hide. I did not have the dog along and did not want to spend all morning looking for a wounded duck. So I took off after him. Gun in hand, bent over, staying just below the worst of the branches and sharp sticks, going as fast as I could. My hat was bearing the worst of it, and I saw that I was gaining on him. Just a little bit more and—THUD. Stopped dead in my tracks, butt on the ground, sitting there, my head spinning, eyes crossed and not sure what had just happened.

I grabbed the frayed bill of my cap in the motion of taking it off and wiping my brow. But my hat would not come off. I pulled and pulled. Nothing. My hat seemed to be stuck. I felt the top of the hat and there was a piece of thorn sticking out of it. My hat was stapled to the top of my head with a locust thorn!

NEVER EAT STINK BAIT

I snapped up the gun and resumed my hunt with renewed vigor.

Walking back to the road, duck in hand, my head began to throb.

When I got back to the pickup, I tried my best to look into the rear view mirror to see this piece of wood that was protruding from my skull, but I could not.

I knew that the Redhead was at church with the passel of kids and the house would be empty. So I drove home and stood in front of the bathroom mirror and tried to come up with a plan to extrude the hunk of wood that was decorating the top of my skull. After all my initial efforts had failed, I had to resort to the fact that I would need help. But worse, I would have to let someone see my condition.

Gar-Bob was the last person I wanted to go to, but I showed up at the fishing shack. After the usual small talk about weather and my trap line, I asked Gar-Bob that if I showed him something would he promise not to laugh. Gar-Bob said, "You and I have been friends long before you made the mistake a'marrying m'sister. You can show or tell me anything."

I took off my hat.

It took a few minutes for the laughter to die out. He wiped the tears from his eyes, caught his composure and said, "You have nothing to fe'r about, the late deer season is just around the corner, but no one is going to shoot you with only that one spike."

I told him to shut up and help me get this thing out. We started simple. He grabbed ahold of it and pulled to no avail. He clamped a pair of brand new, shiny vise grip pliers on it and pulled—still nothing. He said, "I need a little more leverage." He got up on the bench and from above me was able to get a better angle. Gar-Bob pulled again and was still not able to budge the wedged wooden widget. He said, "Grab a hold of someth'n." I placed my hand on the underneath side of the bench. Gar-Bob let out a yell he usually only uses to scare the kids at Halloween with and yanked for all he was worth. There was air between the bottom of my hip waders and the dirty floor, and the only reason he did not pull me up to the top of the bench was the fact that I was holding onto the bottom side of it.

Gar-Bob chuckled, "Maybe you should just comb your hair over it."

I headed back home. As I sulked out of the fishing shack and in between Gar-Bob's hoots of laughter, he kept talking, "Come Christmas you can put a star on it—the 4th of July you can stick a flag on it." I did not look back.

When I got back home, the little woman was there with all the kids. After the usual small talk of weather and how the trap line went this morning, I asked if she would go into the bathroom with me. Now any married man will tell you with kids under foot, romance can take unusual turns, but the wife could sense that this was not one of those special moments. We went into the bathroom and after securely shutting the door, I took off my hat.

I did not tell her, but her "not sure what I am looking at" gaze reminded me of Helda so many years ago. She just stared at it. "Help me get this out before it takes root and starts to grow" I growled. The pounding in my head was getting the best of me. Over the years, I have learned that no matter how bad the situation, aggravating the Redhead isonly going to

NEVER EAT STINK BAIT

make matters worse. I gave her my best puppy-dog-eye look.

She wanted me to go to the hospital. I told her there was no way I was going to the hospital and let my friend Red's wife, the nurse, see this. It was bad enough that Gar-Bob already had seen it. Everybody in town was going to be talking about this tomorrow.

She got a pair of pliers. I told her that we had already tried that. She commented that she was scared that if we did get it out, something dreadful was going to happen. I told her that it was not like oil, nothing was going to bubble out.

She made an unneeded zinger about her agreeing that there was no danger of anything of value—like oil—gurgling out of my head.

She dug around in my tool box and found two pointed leather awls. She helped me poke them into the spike of hardwood. Then I took the handles of the two awls and using the top of my head as the lever and looking into the mirror to guide me, I pulled down. There was the resonating sound of TLUPH, like pulling the cork out of a champagne bottle and voila, Elvis had left the building. I was holding one of the awls with the piece of the woody thorn still stuck to it. It was as big as a pencil and fairly long.

The Redhead demanded, "Put your head down here." She started laughing. She snickered, "I guess everyone has been right all these years, you do have a hole in your head."

I stood back up. The bathroom door was ajar and the whole tribe of kids was gawking at their dad in disbelief. Later on, in their stories to their friends they said they saw Mommy pull the plug out of Daddy's head, but they could not understand why I did not deflate.

There was a writing pen lying on the sink. I took it and put the pointed end into the divot left by the thorn. It fit perfectly and the pen stood straight up and tall just like it was meant to be there. The crater that was created from that encounter lasted quite some time. It was a great party trick for many years.

Later that night the Redhead cooked us a nice meal. The wife and I, and all the dirty-faced kids sitting around the table enjoyed roast duck and all the fixings. The kids all clawed for a piece of the main course like lions at a recent kill.

Myself, I leaned back in my chair, enjoyed each bite of that duck, and chewed real slow.

Country Roads

The airwaves are full of country songs with Nashville's best yearning for their return to the back roads of home. Melodies filled with homesick people longing for and reminiscing about past wonderful down-home memories. That somehow a return to the dusty roads of their youth will make all of life's issues, problems, and stress just fade away like a great military hero.

Well, here in Middle Earth, or as we know it—Nebraska— we only have about a New-York-City-block's worth of population, yet we are blessed with the equivalent of all of Mordor's worth of back roads or better described as minimum-maintenance roadways.

Our local County Commissioners invented minimum maintenance roads because of their sick sense of humor and the fact that they were not allowed to put out police spike strips on the county roads. Minimum maintenance roads were first built as test tracts for military vehicles to assess their longevity and toughness, and out of necessity, here in Nebraska we began to use them as trails and later as roadways for our horseless carriages.

To give these dirt paths vocal, nostalgic, emotional words recalling days of the past is to forget what they are now. These sentimental thoroughfares that have never been disgraced, with rock let alone cement, come equipped with deep ruts left by the last vehicle that slid sideways down them after a summer rain. After these ruts have had time to dry and cure in the sun, they become so hard NASA could use pieces of them as part of the re-entry shields on space shuttles.

No matter how good the ole boys in Detroit originally built my tired old fishing truck twenty years ago, the 300,000 plus miles since then (most of them from driving to church on Sunday) have reduced things like door and window seals to distant memories. Driving down one of these wistful dusty roads is an experiment to measure how much dirt the lungs can endure. Not just any vehicle is up to par for the rigors of backroads USA. To qualify to travel down such a dirt path the participant must own a four-wheel-drive vehicle. I own such a monster. The only problem is, the front driveshaft of my 4x4 is riding in the pickup box with the U-joints out of it, waiting for my next paycheck so I can have enough money to repair it.

Gar-Bob and I drive down these romantic back roads— mostly because it is usually best we stay off the beaten path. Things like brake lights, tail lights, and current license plate tags mean a great deal to some people.

A person would think that driving down one of these back roads would be a trip down memory lane with only you, the road, and the butterflies.

NEVER EAT STINK BAIT

Think again.

The rest of the local populace are driving there as well, kicking up a dust cloud equaled only by what a herd of buffalo could have produced. There are no picturesque panoramic views to see. Matter of fact, I cannot even see the road ahead of me for the mushroom cloud of dust. For the amount of traffic I was encountering, one would think that the end of the rainbow had set just over the next hill and the pot of gold was going to be the prize for traveling down this grimy old dirt trail. But I know that the moment I get the inevitable flat tire, it is like sitting in the Sahara Desert waiting for the next camel caravan to come along.

The words "minimum maintenance" give the illusion that there is going to be at least some maintenance. It is similar to the words in the owner's manual saying my lawn mower only needs minimum maintenance. When I am done mowing, I simply push the silly thing back into the shed. And when it is time to mow again, I reluctantly go get it, and without so much as checking the oil, take off. Minimum maintenance means no maintenance.

As caterpillars turn to butterflies, minimum maintenance dirt roads transform as well. Not to beauty, but to long untraversable expanses of grotesque mud-pie traps, just waiting to lure unsuspecting explorers.

Speaking of mud pies. Who hasn't made mud pies? It is a standard childhood rite and even more fun now to do with my granddaughter because I do not get yelled at for getting dirty, and I can send the granddaughter home to get cleaned up. If one has not made mud pies, it is a pretty easy recipe to follow. It requires dirt and water. If you have a dirt road that gets rained on—voila!—you have a long stretch of mud pies laid end to end as far as you can see.

When this situation happens, it is a signal to every young boy with a pickup truck and big tires that it's time to express his manliness and see how far he can drive down into this quagmire. I have to admit that I was once afflicted with this need to show the world and the pretty girl sitting next to me that "I can do this." Of course, most lassies lose their smiles after they have walked a mile through the knee-deep sludge of the nostalgic dirt boulevard to get back to the county rock road. The thrill of triumph when slip-sliding through a stretch of muck and mire and not getting stuck lasts only as long as it takes to tell all your friends about your accomplishment—but the ruts you left will keep on providing pain to the explorers to come. Until next year.

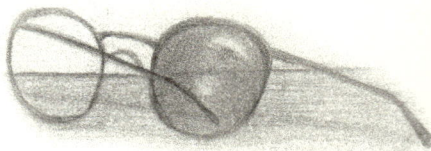

Once these ruts cure, they become the first known use of "no-hands steering" technology. I was driving down one of the dirt roads that had contracted the disease of rutting, and no matter how hard I tried to stay out of the rut, I unavoidably ended up in the crevice, going wherever it guided me. I could let go of the steering wheel because the vehicle went wherever the rut went. If the last person who drove down this path had gone off into the ditch, then that is where the ruts went, and that is where I went too.

Once, after a cooling summer sprinkle, Gar-Bob and I were headed to one of our favorite fishing holes. All of our favorite fishing holes seem to be at the end of one of these so-called

NEVER EAT STINK BAIT

"memory-filled" dirt lanes. Did I mention the cooling summer sprinkle? As we started down the road and the ole pick'm-up truck was sliding sideways, even Gar-Bob was questioning the intelligence of our decision. The stick-on dashboard compass was showing north, then south, and then back north again right before it violently broke off and fell to the floor where Gar-Bob was hiding. But the driving skills I had honed over the years of motoring down these nostalgilistic (a new word I just made up to describe a wash-boarded, rutted-up, mud-infested road), fickle dirt highways allowed me to navigate and keep going, even though only two wheels were propelling us along. (Remember the driveshaft.) I told Gar-Bob to get back up off the floor and help yank on the steering wheel because right beside the 4x4 driveshaft lying in the pickup box was also the broken power steering belt.

As we finally made our way to the top of the high spot in the road, we knew that we would be OK. As we crested the hill, we were met with the view of the forested glen, mist coming off the pastures, with deer and turkey standing along the road, just like the song said. But the words in the ballad did not give a full description of what Gar-Bob and I were seeing, which was the next long expanse of the nightmarish mucky-murky-muddy lane that led up the next hill to where the gravel started again and a pardon from this back road dungeon.

I couldn't let Gar-Bob see the fear in my eyes, so I reached down and picked up my broken sunglasses off the dirt-encrusted floorboard.

Now that you have the recipe, you have dirt until you add water, and then it becomes mud pie. I hung the glasses on my nose, and put them on over my "eye", as only one lens of the sunglasses was left. The compass falling from the dashboard had broken the other lens out. Gar-Bob latched onto the dash and clamped down. I can still see the divots in the dash. I stomped on the gas pedal and away we went, engine blaring, the last surviving belt on the engine squealing, and Gar-Bob and I screaming at the top of our lungs. Down the hill we went, all the critters gone from view. If animals could laugh, I am sure they were hiding under cover, snickering to themselves.

Gar-Bob and I were encouraged by the speed and headway we were making, forgetting about the nerve damage we were going to have from being whipped back and forth as the pickup slid to and fro. People at the county fair would pay for such a ride. All of our success came to a screeching halt once we headed up the next hill. Forward progress terminated as the mud gripped the tires so tightly that nothing the engine and the two back wheels could do would break us free.

There we sat.

But a plan came to us. Now it is common knowledge amongst our friends and family that when Gar-Bob and I come up with a plan, it is time to leave the room and get as far away from us as you can.

One of us would get on the back bumper and jump up and down to give the back tires more traction. Gar-Bob really liked the idea until it dawned on him who was going to be the one jumping on the end of the plank.

NEVER EAT STINK BAIT

So, with Gar-Bob in place, I threw the pickup in reverse, and started plowing our way backwards. As I guided us rearward, I could see Gar-Bob's face in the rearview mirror. Remember the look on the Sherriff's face the first time he saw *Jaws*?

To give ourselves as much of a running start as I could, I backed up the hill as far as the mud would let us go, and it was like the bell went off at the Kentucky Derby. Dirt (mud) going everywhere, Gar-Bob jumping up and down on the bumper, the tires getting a bite now and then, the pickup starting to gain speed as we motored down the last part of the downward slope, and then started our climb up the hill. I could see gravel getting larger in the windshield. I could only see through the windshield part of the time, as the pickup was bouncing so hard it was like riding a raging rodeo bull. But I had a steering wheel to hold onto—Gar-Bob only had the top of the tailgate. I can understand his fear as well as the impression in the dash he left, but I can still see his fingerprints in the tailgate where he was holding on, too.

There was a major jolt, one last Herculean bounce of the vehicle, and we straightened out and we seemed to be on our way past minimum maintenance to a gravel roadway. Looking back in the rearview mirror, I could no longer see Gar-Bob on the bumper. Then I saw him— back there—quickly getting smaller in the rearview mirror, lying on his back, his face tattooed with the thick muck thrown his way from the tires, marooned in the middle of the muddy abyss.

Now, the decision. The pickup was moving, freed from the mud prison. To stop would mean being stuck again. Continuing on, I would sentence Gar-Bob to a long uphill stroll, ankle deep in muddy purgatory. I stomped back down on the gas pedal. From where he was standing, I was confident he could not see the grin on my face.

I waited at the top of the hill, sitting pretty on the foundation of the hard gravel road under me. After Gar-Bob got in and his wheezing quit, he gave me a look that did not inspire friendship.

I said, "You could have at least cleaned off your boots before you got in."

His lips firmed up, his eyes squinted, his forehead wrinkled up and he said, "I could see y'r smile in the rearview mirror."

I'm sure Gar-Bob holds no melancholy recollection or nostalgic memories for that miserable stretch of backwoods country road. As a matter of fact, he told me later, "When I got home, smashed every ole record (yes, record) of every song that had anything to do with or said anything about 'country roads back home.'"

New Tires

There comes a time in every young man's life when he makes the decision to face the cold north wind and go out into the world on his own. Strangely enough, that day came to me at the very same time I came home one day to find all my clothes sitting out on the back porch of my parents' house. My mom said that she was not kicking me out, and that I was free to sleep in the wood shed out back. Mom also informed me that the room where I had spent my first 17 years thinking about all that I was going to accomplish in my life, was soon to be an exercise room, and there was no longer a place for me here in this establishment.

Uh, I thought. That's good. It was time, just as Rudolph being banished from the North Pole, to set out on my own. This world doesn't look all that hard to navigate. I was armed with the same fortitude that all fledgling mentally-undeveloped people possess. My mind held the answers to all the questions of any meaning and was oblivious to all the other issues that I had no clue about. I was impatiently ignorant and mindlessly misguided and confident that the world was going to bow at my feet out of respect for my abilities and qualities.

So, with no fear—and obviously no knowledge—of what lay in wait for me, I loaded (needing only a small cardboard box) all my worldly possessions into my old Chevy, quarter tank full of gas, station wagon. I drove off into the sunset, ready to conquer the world, sitting proudly upon my four bald tires.

In no time, I surmised I was going to be requested to Washington to assume the new position of Commander. All I had to do was work around the apparent logistics of having no money, no plan, no place to live, and the most prevalent problem of not having an income-producing job. All simple obstacles that I would overpower with my profound, youthful, before-my-years wisdom.

In no time at all, I was employed in an executive position in the energy field. I was excited, as it was going to be a great experience to deepen my empathy and my much-needed understanding for the common people. I was sure in the knowledge that I was soon to be moving up the ranks and into a place of status. My new job allowed me to speak to the rank and file about their drab lives as I filled their gas tanks with liquid propellant.

The accumulation of wealth I was rapidly amassing allowed me the privilege of eating one very satisfying meal once a day. Most other civil liberties I had known as the resident of my bill-paying-parents' home were now no longer freedoms I indulged in. As time when on, some luxuries just fell by the wayside. Who needs socks anyway? I had shoes. Clean underwear is really only for the ultra-rich. And, tires that are adorned with extras such as tread, were only needed by people who did not possess my driving skills.

My uncle owned a car mechanic shop in town, and every morning I would stop in his shop to talk, discuss world events, and fill all my four black rubber balloons, and the extras I carried around for safety requirements in the back of the station wagon, with O_2. On most days as well, I would have to repair one or two of my tire wannabes with a patch or two. Some of my tires had accumulated enough patches that they now had another complete layer of protection from the tire-puncturing projectiles that adorned the roadways I traveled. With everything aired up and properly patched, I would head off to work singing as happily as one of the dwarfs looking for Snow White. On occasion (and by "on occasion" I mean most days), I stopped midway to my new-found station in the world's marketplace to enjoy the world around me. This was an important part of growing into my place in the realm of things, and it also gave me time to change the flat tire with another black, round, soon-to-be-flat spare.

After a hard day of helping the worker bees of the world with their petrol needs, ridding the world of kamikaze bugs off all the windshields I came into contact with during the day, I was ready to make the trek back home. With ritual efficiency, I would restore the bounce in all my tires and spares and then begin my journey. There were even times, given how much extra atmosphere I put in the tires, I would make it all the way home before I would have to stop and replace one or two of them.

Not too long into my employment, upper management soon realized their use of their most valuable, and quite possibly, their best asset, spending the day out on the drive dispersing gasoline was a huge misallocation of resources. So, I was asked to come inside and become part of the executive team. In my new position, I was still gainfully employed as part of the oil business, but now was given the task of releasing the spent oils and lubricants. After I had sufficiently mined all the used oil I could get out of the holding reservoir, I would rejuvenate the Henry Ford's internal combustion engine with new liquid gold petroleum. I would even top off the process with a new oil filter as well. I felt as if I was working hand in hand with Henry himself.

The first Friday after my employment progression, I was ecstatic to learn that my advancement came with monetary growth as well. Well, it was about time. I was on my way. Maybe I would buy a new house, go on an extended vacation, or just start thinking about retiring altogether. After the initial shock about all the money I was now making subsided, my eyes made the way to the bottom of my pay voucher, and found that the increase in my gross income was mirrored by the amount of capital I was being asked to help fund the government. I guess I had to learn about the real world sooner or later. You'd think a person's parents would have warned them of such things.

I spent the evening thinking about how to invest my newfound prosperity. Maybe a pack of tube socks, maybe that second meal for the day I have always dreamed of, or maybe, just maybe, I could think about the idea of purchasing some new black rubber air-holding apparatuses—new tires.

So, it came to be that I was the owner of a complete set of non-radial, two-ply, straight-tread, Goodyear's "best"— new TIRES. I held back enough money that I was able to put almost a half tank of gas in the ole station wagon, just so I could drive a couple of extra trips around town. People stopped and stared as if I was the emperor with new clothes.

This was late fall. The next morning came a heavy frost. I was a little late for work and driving at an accelerated rate of speed, but equipped with my artificial youthful intelligence, I knew that I was going to be able to handle any situation that might confront me. Besides, I was riding on four fully aired and ready-to-go straight-tread tires that would follow my every instruction.

As I herded the station wagon down the roadway, thinking maybe the next large increase in pay I could address the worn-out steering tie rod ends, another late-for-work individual backed out of their driveway with no regard for the others on the road.

It might have had something to do with my never yet had an accident Mario Andretti speed, or worrying about what radio station was playing, but the station wagon and I were on a direct course that soon was going to intersect into the rear corner of this car. The collision siren was blaring loudly in my head.

With a firm grip—my fingers were clamped onto the steering wheel with force enough to leave marks—I casually—and by that I mean frantically—cranked the steering wheel as far as it would go to the right, as hard and fast as I could. I reinforced this skillful driving motion with a loud announcement of words that was heard for blocks in the surrounding neighborhoods. I then masterfully yanked the steering wheel back to the left to bring the vehicle back to its original course.

My new tires performed beautifully. They obeyed the first command without a question. The second command... not so much. The icy film that was covering the roadway was more than a match for my new non-radial, two-ply straight-tread, Goodyear's "best" (translation: cheapest) New Tires.

The station wagon and I kept right on going and going and going, to the right. The station wagon and I were launched up and over the curb, out into the back lot of the local Oliver tractor dealership, where they had a display of this year's new model of grain headers sitting on the ground. They were yet to be fully set up and were not yet adorned with the grain reel. But the sickle bar was installed and quite sharp. The station wagon and I hit with a resounding thud squarely in the middle of the grain header.

I inspected the damage, found two sickle sections had given their lives to the cause. The result was my two front non-radial, two-ply, straight-tread, Goodyear's "best" tires were filleted in half, right down to the rim.

Once again, on my way to work every morning, I was able to pause and enjoy the world around me, as I changed one or both of the front tires with a still-aired-up spare from the back.

I have long since moved past the trials of youth. I have graduated to graying hair and a permanently sore back, and on to a period of my life where I am less sure of things than I once was. But I also have gained the knowledge and insight of experience which were lacking in my younger self. Since that time there have been many new tires that have come and gone in my life. I also have come to realize that life is fleeting. What you are confident of right now could easily be erased by tomorrow. Be thankful today, for whatever tires you have in your life.

BRYAN MELLAGE

What do tail feathers look like?

People say they golf to relax. So why are there expensive-looking drivers wrapped around the trees on the fairway? Personally, I pheasant hunt to relieve life's anxieties.

It had been a long week at work. The weekend has come and pheasant season is still on. I think I will go to the country and unwind with a nice walk in the Great Outdoors pursuing Sir Pheasant.

I put a few shells in the pockets of my weathered, but faithful hunting jacket. If you look up "few" in the dictionary, it says, "not very many." My wife, who just by coincidence has beautiful bright red hair just like Mr. Roo, cannot understand why I have to carry a couple boxes of shotgun shells if I am just going out for a short time. What if I am descended upon by a flock of rabid pheasants and I need to defend myself? She just does not understand pheasant hunting. Besides, I need that many shells to offset the weight of all the other equipment I have in the other side of the vest. NFL players working out carry less lead and dead weight. But to hunt this majestic bird requires a person to be prepared.

Before I get off the porch, many of my needed shells have been deposited onto the floor. Only then did I remember about that barbed wire fence that tore a gaping hole in the pocket of my crappy old worn-out hunting jacket last time out. No big deal, nothing a little gray tape will not fix. Repair is done—we are ready to go.

My hunting boots have walked many a mile, as have the shoe filaments—it has been a long time since they were strings—which are due to be replaced. I should do that someday. I pull the boots on, and one good jerk is all that is needed to break the weakened threads of one of the shoe filaments. UGH. Well, the strings do not need to go all the way to the top. Mr. Longtail does not know about shoe strings.

I get out my ole friend. That Ithaca model 37 has been with me for many years, longer than I have been with my wife, and I can tell it things I would not dream to tell her. It shows the weathering of countless trips to the forest floor. Many times it has shown its valor of sacrifice, taking one for the team and protecting me from sure-fire injuries.

The rubbed-clean-of-varnish stock shows the dents that would have been the scars in my forehead. The bluing on the barrel is long gone and has been replaced with pockmarks of surface rust. I have some of the same markings, but on Sean Connery and myself they are called "character features." The zipper on the leather gun carrying case has not worked for years. I step over the trash on the back porch that my wife has asked me repeatedly to take out—and by asked, I mean threatened me with removing my eating privileges unless I

NEVER EAT STINK BAIT

do it. Front of the gun case goes up, and the gun slides out the unzipped back end of the case. THUD. What's another ding in the stock? The pheasant flying hard to avoid me does not care how pretty my gun is.

Yes dear, I will take the garbage out to the curb when I get back.

I let the dog out and get in to start the pickup. That faithful hunting chariot rests patiently all week just waiting for me to show up. CLICK CLICK CLICK. Battery is deader than the three-month-old, mushy jack-o-lantern decomposing on the front porch.

Hook up the battery charger.

I had forgotten the dog collar, so I go back inside. Yes, dear. After I get done taking the trash out, the battery is charged up. Then I'll be ready to go.

Dog loaded and we are off. Flop Flop Flop. Ten yards into the hunting trip the problem is obvious—flat tire. The Redhead standing at the back door laughing at me is my first clue she is not going to help.

Little air in the tire, and we are under way.

With all the prehunt activities, I had not noticed the friendly breeze that had been blowing from the south had swung around and morphed into a northern blast that originated far above the Arctic Circle. Heading out of town, driving south, I had not detected what the wind Was carrying with it—humidity.

I pull off the main road, just a little more, and we are there. Sitting in the pickup, I can see the Promised Land: a long line of heavy grass leading up to a large area of cattails completely surrounded by crop land, all lying in a northerly direction from the road. Food, cover and water. That is Hotel Pheasant.

I get out of the pickup and the heavenly North Wind promptly sends my hat flying south.

I let the dog out, load the gun and gaze toward the North Pole. Glasses fog up. The little pellets of humidity hitting my face feel like a Saharan sand storm.

It takes a strong-willed man to hunt the king of the winged birds.

I remind myself that Grandpa always said, "Hunt into the wind." I wish Grandpa was here; I would stand behind him.

The dog is staring at me with a look of "Are you kidding me?" I encourage him—ok, bribe him—with a treat. From one hunter to another, no matter how hungry you are, do not eat one of those dog treats.

The county road has been built up pretty well here. One step off the gravel road… and the next thing I remember is being face down in six inches of snow. What's another blemish on the gun stock and character mark on the forehead?

Always make sure you button your hunting jacket all the way up to the top before you begin your hunting excursion. I dig the fresh, clean, white, wet, miserable snow out from around my neck.

There is nothing like a, stress-relieving pheasant hunt.

I jump into the grass and lean forward the proper geometric angle to lessen the brunt of the hurricane winds and yet not fall over. This does not allow me to see anything except the top of my untied, ill-equipped boot flopping around. The snow on the ground has found this gap in my personal outer force field. Snow in one's boots does not stay

NEVER EAT STINK BAIT

snow for long. This type of humidity melts, and the cold sogginess is beginning to reach my ankles.

As we get to the cattails, the dog gets the scent of our quarry. He is working hard, and we are sure to see what we have come for.

The dog swings and locks up. Solid. There is something right in front of him. I have the same issue. The scruffy branches of a height-challenged deformed tree are between him and me. KAU KAU KAU. The pheasant is making his break for freedom. His instincts and learned experience includes knowledge of wind currents. Mr. Rooster is up into the wind stream and is at supersonic speed in just seconds. I swing my trusted gun right up to the point of being deadheaded in that little tree. I squeeze the trigger. The report of the gun has no effect on Uncle Ringneck. He is heading south for the winter—and fast. I shot way behind him.

God has spent a lot of effort in the creation of the heaven and earth. Yet I am hoping no one will notice the huge gaping hole I just blew in the big beautiful sky.

Now, I'm a pheasant hunter from way back. With the calm of years of experience, I pump out that store-bought spent shell and ram home the next missile out of the magazine. A pheasant projectile of my own making; a combination of secretively selected powder and shot that has brought down many a bird. A ballistic recipe so hush-hush that my kids will not know it until it is bequeathed to them in my Will.

I calmly line him up. Kaboom… and nothing. I missed—again. Dog is looking around and waiting for the "Dead Bird" command. But no, I missed. The last thing I saw of him was his long, colorful tail feathers as he crested the far hill, probably headed back to Asia and where he came from.

Well, something has gone awry with the Force. I check for the obvious: the barrel of this miserable OLD gun I carry around must be bent. I forgot to load shot in the shell. Someone put a trick shell in the gun. UGH!

We trudge back to the pickup and head home with nothing to show for our adventure except the stinging in my almost-numb fingers and my icy wet toes. The cold of the wind seems to be much worse now. Who cares about a stupid pheasant anyway? They sell whole roasted chickens at the store.

Later that evening, while sipping on a corn-soaked libation, relaxing in the warmth of my easy chair, I look up at the portrait hanging on the wall. It is a Norman Rockwellian reprint from the last local Pheasants Forever banquet showing the picturesque scene of hunter, dog and pheasant on wing.

I squint, look hard at the picture. I cannot tell, but it looks like a gun barrel wrapped around a tree.

The Great Wood Tick Festival

There are those among us who believe that the people who are employed by the government must have a personal defect. Not to discredit anyone, but I myself in times gone by, have had this same thought.

As with government jobs and many things in life, there is always another side to the story. A turning of the stone, an awakening to a new day and the inevitable coming of age. Like when I realized that my parents were right about almost everything I accused them of being wrong about.

As a young lad, I had a tremendous problem closing doors, lids and drawers of anything that I had opened. I was about countertop-high one wonderful lazy hassle-free day (wasn't being a kid great?) in the kitchen with my mother in the next room, dutifully sewing up the holes in the knees of my jeans. Poor Mom, I could wear right through any patch she could put on them in a matter of days.

On a seemingly minute-to-minute basis, Mom was always, as she said, "Asking nicely" for me to close the drawer or lid of whatever I was rummaging through. My mom is showing signs of mental instability, so I will be polite and agree with her, but in reality, her "asking nicely" resembled Mr. Limpet's voice after he turned into a fish. My mom's holler could sink a submarine just as easily as Mr. Limpet. Sorry to all you young'uns for that old movie reference—Google it.

The whole idea of closing a door was confusing to me. I mean really, it was summer and hot out; leaving the refrigerator door open just made sense. Why not cool off the great outdoors?

So, I was in the kitchen and on my tiptoes, could just look over the edge of the drawer into the silverware stash and grab a spoon. My mom, with her super-special sensitive hearing, heard the rustling of the silverware. Mothers can feel vibrations of a kid who is doing something they shouldn't be doing as well as a catfish can sense the movements of an injured fish.

NEVER EAT STINK BAIT

Mom yelled at me to come into the next room, and with the swiftness of the roadrunner running from the coyote, I was standing in front of her. Mom asked if I had closed the silverware drawer. How she knew I had opened the drawer in the first place remained a mystery to me until I watched my own wife spawn these same motherly super powers as our kids tried sneaking around behind her back. These same powers also work on husbands—who knew.

With the look of youthful innocence and total disregard of the truth, I said, "Yes, Mom, I closed the drawer." And like a wisp of smoke, I was gone, around the corner and with all the speed a ten-year-old could muster, I ran—eye first— right into the corner of the silverware drawer I had left open.

In an instant, my ever-caring Mother was standing over me as I lay there crying. She stood there with her compassionate eyes and loving presence and said, "I told you to close the drawer."

From that eye-opening moment, which is ironic because my black-and-blue eye was swelled shut for about a week, I learned the other side to the story: Always shut the door, lid or drawer of anything that I have opened.

These lessons of life have served me well here in the southeast corner of the great state of Nebraska. I live close to a state park that sits along the Missouri River, with rolling hills and ancient forests of old growth oak trees. The forest floor is littered with a millennia of dead and dying debris. This is the perfect growing material for the prized fungus of choice, the morel mushroom. The hills and valleys of the park are some of the best places around to find and gather a mesh bag full of morels.

BRYAN MELLAGE

This is not lost to the hordes of novice morel hunters that show up and pick the mushrooms that I should be harvesting.

The only thing more abundant within the park than the outdoor skill-challenged city folk stubbing around in the park's forest is the army of wood ticks that are waiting for them.

Ticks climb to perches in trees and bushes, and when sensing a victim, whether it be man or beast beneath them, they release themselves from their ambush site to latch onto their prey.

Now the people in charge of the park are government employees, and to my original thinking worked there because of their inability to find a real job. Every year, to encourage park visitation, the park management puts on a Spring Mushroom Hunt. The mushroom hunt is promoted as a great family adventure. The government park employees always have the yearly mushroom hunt early in the spring and by early, I mean, way too early. Again fostering my belief that the government workers do not have a clue. Most years, the park's Spring Mushroom Hunt is weeks before the true mushroom season begins, and the masses of outdoor novice city people that show up leave with empty mushroom sacks and are twitching with the creepy crawly feeling of ticks running around in the private parts of their bodies. This has prompted many participants to rename the annual spring event The Great Wood Tick Festival.

This only gave fuel to my thinking that the government employees who managed the park were individuals that are, shall we say, not the sharpest arrows in the quiver. This was brought to a conclusion for me when a couple of weeks after

NEVER EAT STINK BAIT

the waves of unsuccessful mushroom hunters had stomped every inch of the park, we would get the inevitable spring rains and warming of the sun that would produce the condition of Mushroom Aquarius.

There I was, out there after the Great Wood Tick Festival had already occurred, picking gigantic easily-seen forest fungi food. I ran into many of the diminished-mental-capacity government park employees doing the same thing I was doing—picking mushrooms. If they knew that this was the best time of the season to find mushrooms, then why did they schedule the Great Mushroom Hunt so early?

It was as if I had just hit the silverware drawer again. It was, "Duh, I could have had a V-8." It was the bright light, like when the black darkness of the moonless night was transformed by the spotlight the Game Warden was shining on me.

My eyes are now open to a new realization. These individuals were not dull, unimaginative people stuck in a dead-end government job as I had once thought. These people were intelligent, forward-thinking individuals who saw a problem and had come up with a brilliant solution.

How would they be able to pick mushrooms and not have to worry about ticks? As government employees, the most obvious plan would have been to make a study that would involve millions of dollars, Congressional hearings, and take decades to get any results. Or, mastermind a Spring Mushroom Hunt.

Unsuspecting city dwellers show up, wander around for hours, drag their kids kicking and screaming, have their quality family time, leave the park mushroomless and as blood donors for the park's ticks.

BRYAN MELLAGE

Then the genius of their plan was in full view. These brainy, problem-solving, progressive (sneaky) government employees can then pick mushrooms in the quiet of the park, except for the noise I am making, knowing the park has been gleaned clean of blood-thirsty ticks.

The sun has broken open the seal, and a new day has been born. My hat's off to you, Mr. Government employee!

Circle of Life

The sun was still hours away from breaking the grip that darkness held over the land. I stood at the rear door of the houses or more accurately, leaned on it with my eyes closed. Years gone by, early mornings were greeted with my feet hitting the floor, my body bubbling with renewed daily exuberance. I even leapt out of bed, ready to go on work days—but would bolt out the door like lightning on the weekends to take the field to go hunting.

As a young boy, I spent my summers living with Grandpa and Grandma on the farm. Grandpa, the old German farmer he was, would kick the end of my bed around 4:00 every morning. After dragging me down the stairs, out of the house we would go to start chores.

"Grandpa, it is still dark," I pleaded with him.

Grandpa's reply was that if I got up early every day, I would get used to it, and pretty soon would not be able to sleep in past 4:00.

In Grandpa's honor, in my adult years, I have always been an early riser—not a 4:00 in the morning person, but earlier than most people. More often than not, I am able to watch as the sun awakens the rest of the world.

But that was a bushel basket full of used-up calendars ago. Long gone are my days of morning excitement and enthusiasm.

So here I was, more asleep than conscious. No exuberance in my jump; no pep in my step. The blood slowly being pumped through my veins is only moving about the speed of the flow of a stagnant, back-water slough choked with moss. I could hear the sexy sultry sighing voice of my warm bed beckoning me to come back upstairs. Funny, but I heard no such sounds from the wife. Matter of fact, the only thing I got from her was, "Don't get cold!" as she rolled over in bed snickering to herself.

It was opening day of the rifle deer season.

If I wasn't anticipating my daughter showing up here any minute to pick me up, I would surrender my sentry guard post, holding up the porch door, and crawl onto the pile of dirty clothes lying in front of the washing machine and go back to sleep.

My wife, the Redhead, and I have four children, all with distinct personalities and preferences. The last one of the bunch, the one who I am waiting for this morning, is the daughter that every hunting dad dreams of.

She caught her first Master Angler bass when she was six, and got her first camouflaged pump BB gun when she was seven. She has walked with me through endless tracks of timber, miles along meandering creeks and has been my trusty hunting and fishing companion for most of her twenty years.

NEVER EAT STINK BAIT

So here I was, inside, warm, and waiting for her so we could begin the day looking for Mr. Whitetail.

Outside, it was quite a few degrees below being miserably cold. I could feel the icy sting trying to creep through the unsealed edges of the doorway. The Redhead harped on me about resealing that door most of the summer, but I had not figured out how to do it with a fishing pole in my hand, so it would just have to wait until next year now.

As I waited, with my head propped up against the door, my eyelids slowly sliding shut, I began to drift off into that way-too-early-to-be-awake dreamland.

My mind floated off to a time when the kids were young. Whenever I was in the field, I was always followed by one or two of the children. This was inevitable because as I tried to quietly sneak out of the house, the Redhead would grab one of them—usually the one who was in trouble with Mom—and say, "You go with your father," as she jostled them out the door toward me.

My theory of child rearing was that if you are with me, you better keep up. I could be out mushroom hunting with a couple of them apathetically trailing behind me, whining about the thorns, the bugs, or that I was going too fast—and as hard as I tried, I could not shake them. They were like chewed bubble gum you can't get off your finger.

My goal was to continually walk faster than them and get out of earshot of the constant drone of complaints. This only resulted in increased volume of their grumblings as their little legs strained to keep up. I did not bother glancing back to see if they were keeping up, knowing that their survival instincts would eventually kick in. Weird, but they were always right behind me when we got back to the pickup. This only helped to reinforce my theory that my training was working.

As I stood by the door in my semi-asleep coma mode, a buck deer could have been rubbing the velvet off his newly formed antlers on the boot rack behind me and I would not have heard even a bit of the commotion. But through my diminished, still-slumbering hearing, the ruckus made by my daughter's tuned exhaust coming up the lane was ear opening.

When she was looking for her next vehicle to drive, we helped her look at all kinds, colors and makes of cars. But she wanted a pickup, and a pickup she got. No young redneck boy was prouder of his pickup than she was of hers. Its outer shell was in a constant state of mud-encrusted filth that she seemed to think was a reward for driving down wet, slimy back roads. The pickup box was fully equipped with fishing poles, boots, cooler and a wheelchair. (Some things a father just doesn't ask about.) On occasion, I have seen empty beer cans in there, which I assumed she had picked up from along the road in an attempt to clean up the countryside.

She pulled her hunting chariot right up to the back door. I stepped out into the sharp, crisp morning air, and my first gulp of oxygen got wedged in my throat, frozen solid. I climbed into the pickup and waited for the warm air of the cab to thaw out the solid block of breath obstructing the passageway to my lungs.

It was quite a jolt going from the expensive balminess of the home to the untampered-with great outdoors, and its air-borne floating icicles. The north wind delivered an arctic gust of frigidness brought here especially just for this day.

After a moment or two sitting in the pickup, I was able to breathe again and reported to her, "Kinda cold out."

She nodded her head and agreed, "Ya, a little."

We don't talk much; it's a father-daughter thing.

The pickup roared to life and we were off. I coughed as the blood returned to all parts of my body and the warm air was again smoothly coming and going.

We were headed for a couple of deer stands behind my mother-in-law's house north of town. The bitter blast of cold had brought me to alertness—as a matter of fact, my eyes would not blink. They seemed to be frozen open.

The trip out to the countryside was uneventful. My daughter was intent on getting there and did not say anything. The intoxicating warmth coming from the heater vents was beginning to induce a feeling of slumber, and I wiggled myself into the seat. Then the inevitable feeling of dread started to overwhelm me as we neared our selected spot. Soon I would have to exit this snug paradise and enter the zone of frostbite.

We reached the edge of the timber and the location of our morning hunt. She shut the engine off, we got ourselves organized, and looked at each other with the excitement that only opening day brings.

We opened and closed our doors carefully so as not to make any noise. A couple of inches of hard-crusted snow lay on the ground; the darkness was beginning to surrender to the daily invasion of light. The white snow made it easy to see where we were going and we headed out.

The daughter led the way. I was following and having a hard time keeping up with her pace. She walked ahead and did not look back to see how I was doing.

BRYAN MELLAGE

This is a pretty uncaring attitude of hers, I thought. I could fall, hit my head on the frozen ground, become a frozen popsicle (sorry for the pun), and she would not even know it, or even care.

I wanted to yell at her to slow down, but I knew better. I did not want to lose sight of her and get lost in the early light of dawn. I accelerated my stride a little to catch up and strove to keep pace with her.

My life had come full circle.

Camouflage Up!

I am as guilty as the next man. Face paint on, Mossy Oak from head to toe, tufts of grass stuck in my hat, and shrubbery twist-tied to all my extremities—all this just for a trip to Walmart!

As a collective group, we hunters spend a great deal of time, energy, and the kids' college funds trying to make ourselves invisible to our intended quarry. If this much effort, determination, and money were expended to the front yard, it would be lawn of the month for sure.

Opening day of turkey season. The sun has not yet thought about revealing itself. After adorning my outer façade in the best camo makeover possible, I stand outside waiting for my brother-in-law. Gar-Bob always thought himself the next NASCAR superstar just waiting for his chance. Gar-Bob doesn't just show up—he arrives.

I can hear him coming; it is the same foreboding feeling of an impending earthquake. The ground vibrates as though a T-Rex is coming. Earthworms, shaken from their below-ground slumber, emerge from the soil as he pulls up. Gar-Bob throws out a rope, and I pull myself up and over the Earthmover-size tires into his 4x4 pickup, which just happens to be missing the muffler.

He says, "The pickup has a little exhaust leak. It's on the to-do list."

We roar off in the pre-dawn darkness with all the power and excitement that can only be generated by smashing the gas pedal down as far as the dirt and debris on the floorboard allows it to go. The non-muffled sound resonates throughout the neighborhood, signaling every dog to begin their day, and also to make sure everyone within earshot starts their morning as well. The roar of the free escaping hydrocarbons will be gone within seconds, but the gift of dogs barking will go on for hours.

Gar-Bob says he needs no thank you, "W'rn't fer me, all those people would have slept in this fine Saturday morning. Yer welcome."

As we near the specially-chosen secluded corner of timber—and by near, I mean twenty yards—Gar-Bob stomps on the brakes, or at least the brake pedal, because the brake pads have been gone for quite some time. The squeal of metal-on-metal echoes throughout our hunting spot like a freight train screeching to a stop.

Gar-Bob assures me, "Brake pads are on the list too."

He cranks the steering wheel and the pickup lurches sideways and comes to a stop right before we careen into the continental-drift style crevice along the side of the road that our county calls a road ditch.

NEVER EAT STINK BAIT

The atomic bomb mushroom cloud of dust floats over our preselected pristine hunting wilderness.

We get out of the pickup and Gar-Bob tries to close his door, but the rust in the door hinge hampers his efforts. With Herculean effort Gar-Bob SLAMS the door shut.

"Yah, that's on the list."

Our hunting site is a long draw nestled in between two meandering ridges. The clamor of Gar-Bob's door slamming moves through the gulch and ricochets back and forth off the cliffs, finally cresting the hill before moving on.

The forehead of the sun is beginning to show. The first rays of sunlight shoot across the wooded timber. It is a beautiful sight; we are one with nature. It is as if we are the first men ever to be here. The wild beasts here will have no knowledge of humans.

There is a small breeze. We sense this because the empty beer cans in the back of our hunting chariot clank and clatter as they bounce against the sides of the pickup box like a metal woodpecker.

I put a turkey load into the magazine and, with a nearly inaudible clink, pump the shell into the chamber. Gar-Bob growls, "Be quiet, you want to scare 'em off?"

We make our way down into the wooded realm of the bearded one. We are dragging a fox tail anointed with deer urine. Not because turkeys care one way or another, but because that is the way great hunters camouflage their presence to the wildlife.

After the hike, thirty or forty feet into the vast timbered unknown, we hunker down. With face netting over our blackened faces and scent blocker on our clothes, we snuggle up to a tree so we completely blend in. We are smug in the confidence that our woodland camouflage expertise will hide our existence from any gobbler until after the gun blast.

There is no thought of the fact that Gar-Bob has marked and violated every step of real estate between his pickup and our stand with tobacco spit, his bacon-cheeseburger breath, and that he twice stopped to water the flowers.

Later, I wake up from a mid-morning nap to the sound of Gar-Bob's snoring. We stumble back to the pickup completely baffled as to why we did not see any turkeys. Our camouflage was perfect. We came to the only obvious conclusion—there are no turkeys in this over-hunted piece of public land.

Maybe there is another plausible explanation. Maybe, just maybe, our camouflage was not good enough.

What I would suggest is the notion that all that store-bought camouflage gear is only for looks—it looks great at the annual wild game feed, but is not what is needed to hide ourselves out in the wild. What we really need is to be more like the mayonnaise jar.

Stay with me a minute.

The big game is in the fourth quarter; it is tied, and your team is about to kick a field goal, but there is a commercial time out. Just enough time. You sprint into the kitchen where all the fixings are already out and waiting. Your speed rivals an Indy pit crew. The clock is ticking. All you need is mayonnaise. You open the refrigerator door and—and—and, "Where is the mayonnaise?" You move stuff around, the game is back on, and you begin to panic and start to pull one jar after another out until you finally find the mayonnaise jar.

Now that is camouflage.

The only way to find the mayonnaise jar without any hiccups is to sneak up on the refrigerator from downwind, as not to let the sound get to the mayonnaise. With one quick motion, open the door, reach in, and capture the jar. If you do this correctly, the mayonnaise jar does not have time to move and hide.

Given enough time, the mayonnaise jar will slither sideways and hide behind the pickles. Even though it is taller than the pickle jar, the mayo jar can squat down and make himself small behind those pickles, like a buck deer on opening day slinking down a waterway. The mayonnaise jar is bigger around than Grandma's plum jelly jar, but has the ability to pull in its midsection like a middle-aged man as he walks past a group of women at the ice cream social. The mayonnaise jar makes no noise, no movement; it stays concealed in plain sight. The mayonnaise jar blends in with his condiment surroundings. The mayonnaise jar has conquered camouflage.

So keep your camouflaged clothes, wear them to your kids' t-ball game. Maybe no one will see you as you yell advice to the umpire.

But if you want to go without being noticed by things with feathers and fur in the timber, you must think like, be like, camouflage like… and become one with… the mayonnaise jar.

The Recipe

The season is approaching. That time of the year when consumerism reaches its zenith. From the moment that the Halloween mask is put away until Santa's sled is seen disappearing down behind the horizon, I feel confronted by an ongoing blast of visual bombardment, trying to entice me to spend my last two nickels on the trinket that the commercial says I cannot live without. Every waking minute my ears are ringing with the ring ting tingling of Big Box marketing, trying to hypnotize me and keep me off guard as they slip their hands into my pockets and try to grab my already maxed-out credit card.

Even though the onslaught of Christmas season commercials can have the same effect as a mind-numbing politician's election campaign season can give me, I will choose Christmas over an election every time.

Christmas is the best birthday party of the year. It brings friends and family together. It helps to remind me that there are more important things in my life than the bottom line. The time leading up to and during Christmas seems to rejuvenate me and helps me weather the dull times of mid-winter.

Of all Earthly things to enjoy during the Christmas celebration, enjoying the ongoing Christmas food buffet is one of the highlights. Yes, presents are a joy. Although I have noticed Santa gives a lot of presents to a lot of people at my house, I do not remember his paying for any of them. The look on the little ones' faces when they open the plastic, made-in-a-foreign country, February-trash-can-fodder, toy is enough to make this Grandpa sniffle just a little bit.

Seeing relatives and friends who live in lands far away is always a treat. Of course, that brings to mind another one of the season's joys—that feeling of relief as you put on your make believe sad face and wave them goodbye as they head out the driveway.

But whether it is the gift of a new fishing lure, or seeing the new baby of the family, it is hard to beat the ongoing smorgasbord of holiday food. My wife cooks for hours on end to bake cookies, cakes, pies, and other sugary delights, and the house smells of fresh baked bread. These tantalizing tidbits of non-dieting, plate-filling foods are not available during the other eleven months of the year. For Christmas is the time to blow the dust off the recipe box and get out the index cards that hold the family secrets of food formulas past.

These recipes are closely guarded mysteries of ingredients that my wife had to take an oath of silence to receive them from Grandma in the first place. Why we cannot enjoy these mouthwatering foods during the long time period between the first Christmas commercial and the last bite of rock-hard, fell-behind-the-couch peanut brittle, I do not know. These recipes hold special memories.

At our house we have a tradition of family get - together fish frys. We believe that a family that fishes together will stay together—at least it makes sense with us. The celebrated Birthday Boy himself was surrounded by fishermen. What better thing to do with the family underfoot than to have a fish fry. Good food and a good time. When Santa visits our house, there is no milk and cookies, just fresh-cooked fish.

As Christmas approaches, my mind wanders to a time when I was first introduced to fishing with my grandpa. It started with the recipe: A little oatmeal, cornmeal, a little salt and a dash of vanilla, all in exact proportions. I do not know if fish drool, but if they did, this fish-bait recipe would make them do so. This recipe is so secret that if I did divulge it to you, no one would ever see you again.

I helped Grandpa make this fish bait many, many times during the course of my growing up, but it was not until my adulthood that he gave me the written directions of how to make it. It was a special day in my life. I held in my hand the lineage of our family and a record of our proud past as fishermen. I now was ready to go forth into the world and catch fish.

So as people begin to think about the Christmas season, their minds will recall visions and smells of past family get-togethers. There are those who will be looking forward to presents, putting up lights and the tree and getting all excited thinking about a visit from once-a-year-seen relatives and pinching little kids' cheeks. I myself will

BRYAN MELLAGE

be thinking about an upcoming time when my kids and extended family are hovered around the fish cooker, their noses full of the aroma, impatiently waiting for the first piece of golden-brown-outside and soft-white-meat-inside fish to come out of the hot bubbling peanut oil.

My love of fishing and the knowledge of how to do it came from my grandpa. My grandpa's fish bait recipe, now in my safekeeping, is waiting for the next generation. The family fish-bait recipe keeps me linked to my past and enables me to face the future. On the backside of the card he wrote the recipe on, Grandpa wrote the disclaimer,

WARNING:
If you use this bait, you fish through a crack
in a bridge so they don't pull you in.

I look around the Christmas scene, the blinking lights on the tree, kids trying to break their new toys, frost on the window, *It's a Wonderful Life* playing on the TV, surrounded by family as I enjoy another piece of fish right out of the cooker and think, "Thank you, Grandpa."

Warning

If you use this bait you fish through a crack in a bridge so they don't pull you in.

The backside of Grandpa's official recipe card.

Things I learned sitting on the creek bank

From the very first moment of my entry into this big ole world, when the doctor reared back and smacked my butt, it was obvious to me that life was not going to be easy. The "Good Life" can be a hard row to hoe.

From that menacing initial encounter with the hardships of life and the foreboding of what was to come, I became aware of the need to be a quick study. I was going to have to learn about this thing called life, and I was going to have to do it with some urgency.

The speed of life is one of the first things that I had to learn to deal with. As a toddler and later a teenager, I was not aware of the swiftness of which life was happening. Only now, as a slouched-over scarred-up old fisherman, am I able to look back and shake my head in disbelief that I has gotten here so fast. I thought it was going to take longer to get old.

Growing up, I was like warm putty in need of being shaped and solidified. What I got were my friends. One of the hard facts I learned was that my friends were not always the best source of quality tutoring. Do not get me wrong—I learned a lot from my accomplices in the deeds that have spun untold urban legends—yet most of these teachings came with a trip to the principal's office or worse.

Most help offered to me seemed to be similar in action to what the delivery doctor did to me as my first graduation present—a smack of advice. My parents were dedicated students of this educational and motivational guidance tool. I was quickly schooled in what was acceptable and what was not acceptable behavior in the household.

When I was still a young boy finding my way, my mother got her first set of unbreakable Corelle dishes. As I stood near the back door, drying them for the first time, I asked Mom, "These are really unbreakable?" When that indestructible plate hit the cement of the entryway and shattered into a million pieces, school was open and I was given another one of my invaluable life lessons.

As an adult, I still show the effects of Post-Traumatic Stress Disorder. Whenever I hear the sound of someone taking his belt off, I think that my dad is coming up behind me to continue my education.

Just as a mahout trains his elephant to walk down the jungle path by tapping him on either side of the head with a stick, my parents guided me. My dad wore out a couple of belts, used a timber of tree branches, and put callouses on his hand, providing me with my seemingly endless daily lessons.

NEVER EAT STINK BAIT

As a young boy, fear of falling out of a tree never seemed to be an issue; but when Mom said those immortal words, "Just wait until your father gets home," I knew that another lesson was just around the corner and the true meaning of real terror.

Some of my tutelage came with pleasant memories and no welts. Of these, many and the best of them came after Grandpa said, "Let's go fishing." Countless hours were spent sitting next to Grandpa on the creek bank watching the lazy water flow by, taking in his bits of woodlore knowledge. What I came to understand later was that Grandpa was giving me more than outdoor wisdom. His words provided me with the depth and understanding to handle life's challenges. Those times with Grandpa and his dirt-under-the-fingernail intellect helped to fill the void of what I did not know about life.

As time went on, even after Grandpa had gone on to that great fishing hole in the sky, I still sat on the creek bank to continue my training. One is never too old to sit with a fishing pole in hand and carry on one's education.

What I have gleaned from my travels is the realization that all of life's lessons can be learned just sitting on a creek bank.

Let me explain:

- When the bobber goes out of sight—set the hook.

- When the opportunity presents itself—go for it.

- There are no promises given to you of riches and fame.

- You are obligated to create your own successes.

Sitting on the creek bank doesn't mean that you are given permission to sit and do nothing. Participate, get involved, put yourself in play, and don't allow the fear of failing hold you back. The worst thing that can happen is that you miss setting the hook, and it comes out of the water and gets stuck in the tree behind you. Big deal. If you miss, try again. You will lose every fish you don't try to catch. Get in the game.

- If one type of bait is not working—try another. You cannot expect a different result if you keep doing the same thing. You can see that lunker bass sitting under the lily pad, and you have been throwing that yellow jig at him with no luck. Try a black one and see what happens. Do not be stubborn. Adapt. Take the other fork in the road, and be willing to adjust for the situation. Embrace change.

- When your grandpa is showing you how to tie a hook on—watch and learn. Those old people with wrinkles (like the guy I see in the mirror nowadays) have a lot of knowledge. You are only going to be privy to this information if you are polite and courteous to them and are willing to be taught. Respect your elders.

- Every day of your life is traded for what you did that day—or more importantly, the result of that day. It is the debt you pay for the witnessing of another sunrise and sunset. Make sure at the end of the day, you have made a good trade.

- Not every day has to be a conquering of the neighboring nation. Exchanging an afternoon of your life for a relaxing day of watching the water passing by can be a very good trade. Remember, Jesus was a fisherman. Enjoy the world around you. Take a vacation. Grandpa had a bracket on the side of the Oliver 1755 farm tractor to hold his fishing rods.

- Make good decisions.

- Don't take all the fish home. Just because you have caught them doesn't mean you have to take them home. Be mindful of the next person who might come along after you. Throw some back for him. Don't be greedy.

- Take a friend with you on your next outdoor venture. Take your wife or your girlfriend (never both) out fishing. It is mandatory to take your kids and young'uns down to the creek bank and an absolute must to take your grandkids. That way you get to enjoy the adventure with them. Walking along the creek bank, fishing for bait with my pigtailed nine-year-old niece, she stopped dead in her tracks, looked up and with a face as serious as I had when I told the principal that I knew nothing about the snapping turtle in the school library, she asked, "Are there alligators in here?" We are in Nebraska. Celebrate life with other people and you get to enjoy it twice.

- Buy the fishing gear you need, not what you want. What good is an expensive bass boat if you cannot afford the gas for it? Just because the other guy has prettier equipment than you doesn't mean he is going to catch more and or have more fun than you. A one dollar fishing pole bought at a swap meet will catch a big one too. Learn to live within your means and don't worry about what the other people have.

- Leave the creek bank clean of evidence of your being there. Clean up after yourself.

- This is a hard one: Tell people how big your fish was and not how big you wanted it to be. Tell the truth.

- Be thankful for your catch. Life is a gift, and you should be grateful for every moment you have. Maybe that "catch" was watching a white-spotted deer fawn come down to the water's edge for a cool drink, or the ear-to-ear smile on your granddaughter's beautiful face or the rosy red glow of the sky as the sun slowly slides down beneath the horizon at the end of the fishing trip. Life might seem like one long schoolroom with a long list of homework, but remember this is the only classroom you will ever get. Enjoy and be thankful for the life you have.

So get a can of worms, a cane pole, a bobber and a friend. Slide on down to the creek bank and listen to the crickets. School is open.

NEVER EAT STINK BAIT

Acknowledgments

I would like to recognize many of the people who
have helped me along the way.

To the girls in the writing club for egging me on.

To Gary and all my friends who have had
to live through these "stories."

To my parents who guided me through the years—
or at least tried.

Grandpa, who taught me my love and
respect of the outdoors.

To the Redhead, for so much, but mostly for staying.

Praise God for our wonderful Earthly residence, the
gift of His son, and the promise of an eternal home.

About the Author

Bryan Mellage is a native of Southeast Nebraska, where nearly all these stories take place. He's been married to the Redhead for nearly forty years and is the father of four grown children and Grandpa to four. He's an avid fisherman and hunter, and enjoys sharing his love of the outdoors with his family, especially the grandkids.

Several of Bryan's short stories have been published by magazines, such as *In Fisherman*, *Nebraskaland*, and *Whitetails Unlimited*. He has a unique sense of humor that will tease you into smiles, giggles and outright LOL!

"Enjoy this storytelling adventure from Bryan,
and share the fun!"
—The Redhead —

www.ingramcontent.com/pod-product-compliance
Lightning Source LLC
Chambersburg PA
CBHW022009080426
42733CB00007B/542